LINKAGES

LINKAGES

IMPROVING FINANCIAL MANAGEMENT IN LOCAL GOVERNMENT

Frederick O'R. Hayes
David A. Grossman
Jerry E. Mechling
John S. Thomas
Steven J. Rosenbloom

THE URBAN INSTITUTE PRESS
WASHINGTON, D.C.

Copyright © 1982
The Urban Institute
2100 M Street, N.W.
Washington, D.C. 20037

Note: Copyright is limited to format only. No claim is reserved or implied for the contents
of this volume.

Printed in the United States of America

Kuhlmann-Anderson TestLC 82-60180
ISBN 87766-313-0

Research for this publication was conducted under a grant by the Office of Policy Development and Research of the U.S. Department of Housing and Urban Development. The
substance of such research is dedicated to the public. The authors are solely responsible for
the accuracy of statements or interpretations contained herein.

Distributed by:
University Press of America
4720 Boston Way   3 Henrietta Street
Lanham, MD 20706   London   WC2E 8LU   ENGLAND

THE URBAN INSTITUTE is a nonprofit policy research and educational organization established in Washington, D.C., in 1968. Its staff investigates the social and economic problems confronting the nation and government policies and programs designed to alleviate such problems. The Institute disseminates significant findings of its research through the publications program of its Press. The Institute has two goals for work in each of its research areas: to help shape thinking about societal problems and efforts to solve them, and to improve government decisions and performance by providing better information and analytic tools.

Through work that ranges from broad conceptual studies to administrative and technical assistance, Institute researchers contribute to the stock of knowledge available to public officials and private individuals and groups concerned with formulating and implementing more efficient and effective government policy.

Conclusions or opinions expressed in Institute publications are those of the authors and do not necessarily reflect the views of other staff members, officers, or trustees of the Institute, advisory groups, or any organizations that provide financial support to the Institute.

USER REVIEW
COMMITTEE

During the preparation of this publication, the authors benefited from the advice and assistance of a User Review Committee composed of the following persons:

Ellen M. Bozman
Member, Arlington County Board
Arlington, Virginia

Gerry D. Brighton
Professor of Accountancy
University of Illinois
Urbana, Illinois

E. O. Coli
Director of Finance
City of Sunnyvale
Sunnyvale, California

Clifford W. Graves
Chief Administrative Officer
County of San Diego
San Diego, California

James Griesemer
Village Manager
Village of Downers Grove, Illinois
Downers Grove, Illinois

Professor Regina E. Herzlinger
Harvard Business School
Harvard University
Cambridge, Massachusetts

Joan Hochman
Vice-President, Citibank Corporation
New York, New York

James A. Hogan
Chairman, State and Local Government Services Group
Coopers & Lybrand
Boston, Massachusetts

Professor Bernard Jump, Jr.
Director, MPA Program
Maxwell School
Syracuse University
Syracuse, New York

Jan Lodal
Executive Vice President
American Management Systems
Arlington, Virginia

Roland M. Malan, Jr.
Auditor, King County
Seattle, Washington

Jerry E. Mechling
Director, Office of Management and Budget
City of Boston
Boston, Massachusetts

Mason Neely
Finance Director
East Brunswick Township
East Brunswick, New Jersey

Lois M. Parke
Member, New Castle County Council
Wilmington, Delaware

William J. Reynolds
Comptroller
Town of Greenwich
Greenwich, Connecticut

Phillip Rosenberg
Assistant Director for Government Finance and Research
Municipal Finance Officers Association
Washington, D.C.

Pamela Syfert
Assistant Director
Budget and Evaluation Department
City of Charlotte
Charlotte, North Carolina

Dan Valdivia
City Auditor
City of Phoenix
Phoenix, Arizona

Edwin C. Whitney
Director, Bureau of Budget and Management Analysis
City of Milwaukee
Milwaukee, Wisconsin

Paul Woodie
Assistant City Manager
City of Dayton
Dayton, Ohio

James Young
Deputy Mayor for Fiscal Affairs
City of Boston
City Hall
One City Hall Plaza
Boston, Massachusetts

Contents

Exhibits

Preface

The purpose of this publication is to set out ways in which financial management in local government can be improved by more effective linkages among the four basic financial management functions. The four functions are

- Budgeting
- Accounting
- Performance Management
- Auditing

The emphasis is on the interrelationships among the four functions. However, effective interrelationships depend on high quality performance of each of the separate functions. As a result, this volume addresses not only linkages among functions but also the standards that should be met in each of the four functions and the ways in which those standards can be met.

Importance of the Objective

This volume is entitled *Linkages* because that is what it is about. It describes how to link together fiscal systems so that they'll work better together.

The need for information on this subject was clearly and emphatically stated at a National Conference on the Financial Management Needs of Local Government. This two-day conference,* sponsored by HUD's Office of Policy Development and Research, took place in Washington, D.C. on June 7–9, 1978. Participants in the conference included representatives of virtually every one of the major national and regional organizations of local officials.

At the conference, participants listed in priority order the needs they felt to be most critical to local financial management. Ranked second among all of the issues listed by the conferees was the need to integrate local budgeting, accounting, auditing, and performance management. The only issue that out-ranked financial integration was the need for better forecasting of revenues and expenditures.

---

*A copy of the final report of the national conference can be obtained by writing: Office of Policy Development and Research, Department of Housing and Urban Development, Washington, D.C.

HUD's Office of Policy Development and Research arranged its work priorities to reflect the concerns expressed by municipal officials at the workshops and in the conference itself. The development of this volume is a direct result of the priority identification at the national conference.

The Office of Policy Development and Research is identifying exemplary cases where local governments have developed innovative and effective methods to link together their financial management systems. Some of these are cited in the text of *Linkages* itself.

The overall objective of this focus on financial management integration is to advance the state-of-the-art of local government finance and management. This is one aspect of the Department of Housing and Urban Development's Capacity Building Program which was founded on the belief that better local management will lead to an improvement in public services and the quality of life.

Organization of this Volume

Linkages is divided into ten chapters which can be grouped into five related parts:

- Chapters 1 and 2 provide an overview for the reader. The first chapter defines an integrated financial management system and explains the benefits that it can provide. The second chapter is a "do it yourself" checklist to let you see where your community stands on the road to fiscal integration.
- Chapters 3, 4, and 5 concentrate on budgeting because we see that as the cornerstone of fiscal management. These three chapters define local government budgeting and explain how it relates to decision making and how it links to the other financial systems.
- Chapters 6 to 9 address the other elements of local financial management; accounting and control; performance management; financial management information systems; and auditing and evaluation.
- Chapter 10 suggests some strategies. It offers ideas on how to go about the process of linking your financial management systems— no matter what point you're starting from.

Finally, the volume closes with a Bibliography that can help you if you want to investigate more deeply any of the subjects discussed in a more general manner in *Linkages*.

How to Read This Volume

How to read this volume varies depending on your own current state of sophistication in local government finance. The authors are fully aware that there are many local officials and legislators who are filling respon-sible positions—and doing it well—who have not had specific financial management training. And, on the other hand, we're also aware that there are many other public officials who have a wealth of such knowl-edge, some of it from prior experience in the private sector. We've tried to present materials in a form that lets you choose your own meal from the menu.

We suggest that everyone start with the overview in chapter 1. It presents the basic idea of integrated financial management. Then, you might want to try chapter 2, a checklist of questions about the financial systems in your community. Your answers to these questions will give you a personal guide to what you may want to know more about.

If you're hesitant about the degree of your knowledge about the fiscal systems of municipal government, read the chapters in consecutive order. You may not be a fully qualified expert on local budgeting after you've finished the three chapters on budgeting, but you ought to know enough to do two things: First, you ought to be able to look at your own locality's budget to see how it compares with what we say are the objectives of local government budgeting. Second, you'll begin to be prepared to see how budgeting *ought* to link up with the other fiscal systems—whether it now does or doesn't in your own local government.

But if you're already knowledgeable about some parts of your local financial management process, you may want to target some specifics. For example, you may want to know more about performance manage-ment (chapter 7) or computerized financial management systems (chapter 8).

Throughout the volume, we've tried to provide illustrations from actual practice to show you both good and bad approaches to fiscal management.

Preparation of the Guide

Linkages was prepared under a grant by the Office of Policy Development and Research, U.S. Department of Housing and Urban Development to Frederick O'R. Hayes Associates in association with the Nova Institute. Its principal authors were Frederick O'R. Hayes and Nova's President, David A. Grossman. Chapter 7 on performance management was written by John S. Thomas, formerly deputy director of the budget in New York City and author of *So, Mr. Mayor, You Want To Increase Productivity.* Jerry E. Mechling, the former director of Boston's Office of Management and Budget wrote chapter 8 on financial management information sys-tems. Steven Rosenbloom of Nova prepared the bibliography.

William Goldstein did much of the initial work in identifying exem-plary practices in many local governments. Professor Donald Simons of the Boston University School of Management served as a consultant on accounting matters. Mary K. Kassler and Emily Shamieh were responsible for work with the User Review Committee.

The staff of HUD's Fiscal Management Capacity Building Program provided highly useful and critical review and guidance. They include Alan A. Siegel, the director of the unit; Hartley Fitts; Paul Epstein; Beverly Beidler; Meg Rorer; and Steven Yedinak.

Credits and Acknowledgments

Local governments in the United States vary enormously—as do their financial management systems. We've tried to write this guide so that it would be relevant to the concerns of the entire range of local government, from the smallest to the largest. We've also tried to write it so that people who aren't fiscal experts can read it.

To the degree that we've come close to meeting those objectives, much of the credit is due to the members of our User Review Committee, the staff of HUD's Office of Policy Development and Research, and the many others who read and commented on this volume in draft.

Frederick O'R. Hayes
David A. Grossman

About the Authors

Frederick O'R. Hayes, a nationally known economist, is currently a public policy and management consultant and director of the curriculum development project in public sector financial management at Boston University's School of Management. He has also been New York City's director of the budget.

David A. Grossman has been the president of The Nova Institute, a nonprofit policy research organization, since 1976. He was deputy budget director for New York City from 1966 to 1970, and director of the budget from 1971 to 1973. He holds degrees in both architecture and city planning from the Massachusetts Institute of Technology.

Jerry E. Mechling is adjunct professor teaching computer science and information systems in the public management program at the Heller School at Brandeis University. He is also a management and computer systems consultant. He holds a Ph.D. from Princeton University's Woodrow Wilson School.

John S. Thomas is an industrial engineer, now with Booz, Allen, and Hamilton in New York City. He was a consultant to the National Commission on Productivity and Quality of Working Life and is a nationally known authority on local government productivity.

Steven J. Rosenbloom is senior associate at The Nova Institute. He has done research and consulting in public sector economics, employment and training, and integrated financial management. He holds a Ph.D. in political science from Columbia University and a master's degree from the London School of Economics.

An Overview of Integrated Financial Management 1

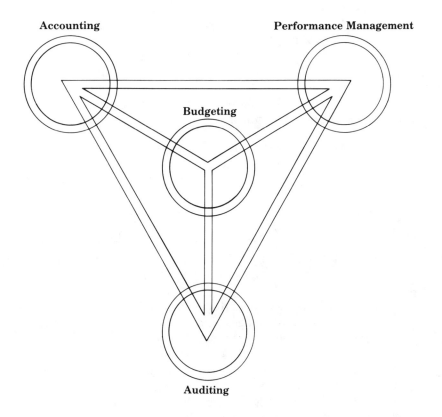

Accounting

Performance Management

Budgeting

Auditing

"better decision making plus effective control"

1

Let's start by addressing the basic question: What is an integrated financial management system? In the way the term is used in this volume, it's made up of four components:

- **Budgeting**—the process of preparing and carrying out a locality's financial plan.
- **Accounting**—the basic financial record-keeping and expenditure control tool of local government and potentially the most valuable information system available to local managers and legislators.
- **Performance Management**—the improvement of public service delivery by establishing and monitoring targets for agency performance. It often includes a focus on increasing productivity.
- **Auditing**—the process of evaluating the locality's fiscal and service operations. Auditing provides vital "feedback" insights for better budgeting, management, and control.

These four components are the heart of the planning and control system through which a local government decides what it wants to do and makes sure that its decisions are carried out or modified to reflect changing conditions. One simple way to look at how the four components are interrelated as parts of the overall planning and control system is presented in exhibit 1–1. The exhibit shows the three basic elements common to *all* planning and control systems:

- **Decision Making.** Planning and analysis are the starting points. They're where decisions are made about what services local government will provide, how much they'll cost, what agencies will do the work, and where the money will come from. Budgeting is the key activity in this process.
- **Implementation.** Management and control refer to the actual operations of government. They're where control systems are needed so that the budget is not overspent and so that managers know what's happening to public services. There are two basic fiscal control systems:
  —*Accounting* reports on actual spending so that management knows if it's sticking to its budget plan.
  —*Performance Management* reports on operations so that local officials know if they're meeting their service delivery targets.
- **Assessment.** Evaluation comes after the fact, to tell local management whether results conformed to its plan. These functions are best met by two types of audit: financial and performance. Both are necessary for full-scale evaluation.

Both implementation and assessment also have an important feedback relationship to the decision-making process.

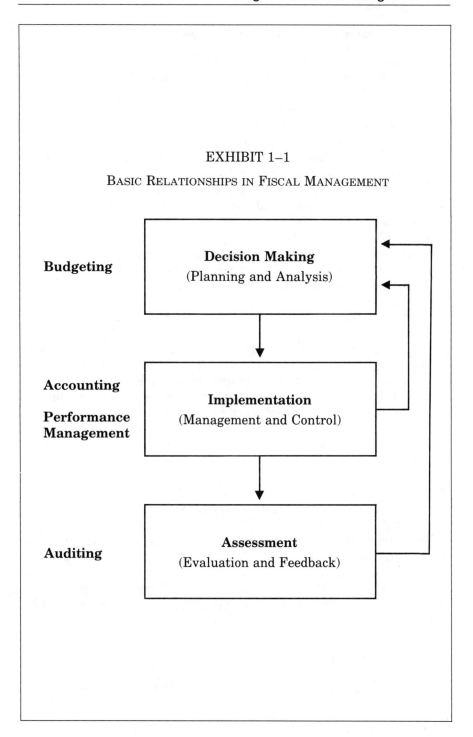

EXHIBIT 1–1

BASIC RELATIONSHIPS IN FISCAL MANAGEMENT

Common Problems of Financial Management

Why is integration needed? In most local governments, the four financial components are not adequately interrelated. The following are common problems:

- The system is fragmented. The budget staff is concerned with budget preparation and expenditure control—but tends to slight the performance aspects of budget implementation. The accountants concentrate on the minutiae of expenditure control. The program administrators do what they have to do and may or may not worry about the effectiveness, efficiency, and quality of program performance.
- Decision making in the budget process is hampered by the lack of adequate information on program performance and results and of financial data that fits budget program categories.
- Administrators are told what they have to spend, and spending limits in most—but not all—local governments are usually observed and enforced. Data on emerging expenditure problems, however, are often not reported promptly.
- Administrators are not usually told what they are expected to achieve in terms of program performance and results. Often, performance is not measured, reported, monitored, or even related to costs.
- Little attention is given by any of the parties involved to the need for interim corrective action to balance performance against costs as the budget plan is implemented and modified.
- The financial system is, in most localities, evaluated by periodic financial and compliance audits. But without independent assessments of program efficiency and effectiveness, programs can be funded and operated without knowing whether they are worth what they cost or whether they could be more efficiently or effectively managed.

These problems are the product of history. Expenditure control has been the dominant objective of local government financial management and the issue of what the public gets for its money has, more often than not, been neglected. The four components have developed largely (but not wholly) as independent systems serving limited, often technical objectives.

Is Financial Integration Feasible?

It is possible to overcome fragmentation and to integrate the four components into an effective planning and control system. We know this because it has already been done in a small but significant number of local governments and because a great many more jurisdictions have made substantial progress toward that objective.

An integrated financial management system is, in fact, more than just a *financial* management system. The result of integrating finances with performance and integrating decision making with implementation is an *overall* management (or planning and control) system.

The breadth of an integrated system is dramatically illustrated in exhibit 1–2, adapted from San Francisco's description of its financial management information and management-by-objective system. While this is an ambitious system, most local governments should be able to achieve many of these same results by using techniques appropriate to their own size and sophistication.

A growing number of local governments have developed or are developing integrated financial management systems. The experience of these governments offers some valuable lessons to others interested in moving in that direction. Several general observations are especially important:

- The support of top management is essential. An integrated system represents not simply a refinement of a technical function but a fundamental change in the way the government is managed. It won't work without the active backing of the chief executive and the support of the legislature.
- An investment of resources in staff, consultants, hardware and software may be necessary.
- A substantial amount of time will be required to do the job or even to complete major steps such as the installation of a financial management information system.
- Some significant resistance within the government can be expected. Integration imposes new burdens on all agencies and increases top management control over both financial and program administration.
- Few of the advantages will come automatically. They depend, rather, on a managerial effort to realize the benefits offered by an integrated system.

An effective integrated financial system can be built only gradually, a step at a time. Some local governments may find it feasible to proceed in fairly large steps while others may conclude that their circumstances dictate a slower rate of progress. Fortunately, the options available are numerous and any local government should be able to develop its own program. Step-by-step progress should yield some benefits with every forward step, even though it may require five to ten years to do the entire job.

Although the development of the financial management system will

EXHIBIT 1–2

FINANCIAL INFORMATION AND RESOURCES MANAGEMENT
(FIRM) SYSTEM: CITY AND COUNTY OF SAN FRANCISCO

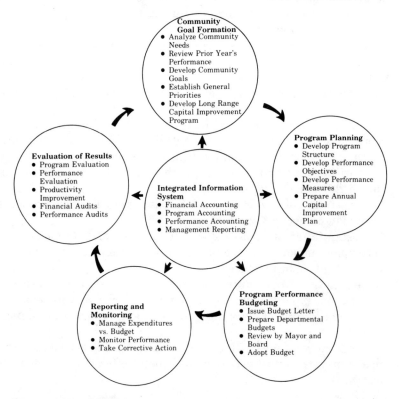

SOURCE: Adapted from figure 5, p. 33 in *Program Measurement Handbook*. Resources Management Program, Office of the Mayor, City and County of San Francisco. February 1980.

require, at some stages, the investment of additional resources and the addition of staff, there are some steps that should involve little or no additional cost. In addition, the prospects are good that the system will generate savings and additional revenues in amounts sufficient to recover the required investment.

Local Governments, Large and Small

The purpose of this guide is to serve all local governments, regardless of size. Officials of larger jurisdictions may find, as a result, that the discussion does not always deal adequately with the scale and complexity of the problems they face. The legislators and executives of smaller jurisdictions may, on the other hand, see the presentation as overly complex in relation to their needs and resources. These problems were inherent in our assignment. A single volume addressed to all American local governments is, necessarily, something of a compromise.

Some of those reviewing the manuscript suggested that the length of the guide and the nature of the presentation were likely to discourage its use by officials from smaller jurisdictions. We hope that this is not so.

Integrated financial management makes sense for any local government whether small or large. Indeed, the most fully developed financial management systems are, with few exceptions, not found in our largest cities and counties. Most are in small and medium-size jurisdictions—in communities like Hanover, New Hampshire, Downer's Grove, Illinois, East Brunswick, New Jersey, and Sunnyvale, California. (Although we have identified comparatively few exemplary approaches in the smallest local governments, this is certainly due, in part, to the fact that progress in those local governments is less likely to receive national publicity and recognition.)

There is a good reason why a significant number of small and medium-size local governments have been able to implement advanced approaches to integrated financial management. The reason is that the obstacles to doing can, often, be more easily surmounted than in the larger cities and counties. In many smaller jurisdictions, a single knowledgeable official— the city, county, town or village manager, or finance director—has been able to initiate and manage the implementation of measures aimed at the gradual development of an integrated system. There is, in fact, no aspect of an integrated financial management system that is not easier to introduce in a small local government than in a large one. With the advent of the microcomputer and software packages, even a computerized financial management information system can be installed in most small jurisdictions in less time, with fewer problems, and, often, at lower per capita costs than in the large cities and counties.

For the very smallest local governments, the integration of, say, budgeting and accounting may be a process that must take place in the skull of a single individual or in the coordination of the practices of two individuals sharing the same office. The officials of such governments will correctly perceive that much of this guide is irrelevant to their needs. Yet, the basic financial management functions, despite differences in organization and scale, are much the same in all local governments. We hope that even for those from the smallest governments that the guide offers some contribution to a sharpened perception of the underlying problems of cost, performance, and purpose.

The Benefits of Integration

Why should a local government invest its energies and resources in the development of an integrated financial management system? The benefits from an integrated system consist, for the most part, of greatly increased opportunities for better decision making, more effective control of both expenditure and performance, and improved program management.

There is no certainty that any particular local government will realize those opportunities—but the local governments furthest along in developing such systems have realized substantial benefits. In those local governments where performance objectives related to the budget have been established for program managers, the managers tend to reason and try to meet those objectives. Ordinarily, they achieve, in the process, some significant improvements in effectiveness, efficiency, and quality of work.

In addition, there are often more certain dollars and cents benefits. The best example is in the claiming of costs under federal and, sometimes, state grant-in-aid programs. Most local governments do not have financial information systems that permit them to determine accurately the indirect costs associated with grant-assisted projects and programs. These costs are, as a result, typically underclaimed. In local governments with large federal grant programs, the increase in reimbursements resulting from a new financial information system will often be enough to amortize the costs of the information system in five to ten years.

Such a financial information system will also generate cost data for programs financed by user charges—such as off-street parking or water supply. Charges in such programs typically fall short of full cost recovery. This may be a policy choice for the local government (some don't want to charge full cost) but an adequate financial information system will provide the information necessary both to define the issue and to justify the charges required to recover full costs.

Almost all local governments are dependent in various degrees on external sources of financing such as grants or loans from federal and state agencies, and the sale of bonds and notes through underwriters. One of the marked trends of the past half-dozen years has been the increase in requirements placed by outside agencies on local financial management practices and reporting. There seems little doubt that this trend will continue, forcing many local governments to upgrade their financial management systems to satisfy grantor agencies or to earn satisfactory credit ratings. Early movement in this direction may earn advantages in interest rates on bonds as well as an easier time with federal and state grantors.

Another important benefit of the integrated financial management system is the discipline of accountability it imposes on both finances and program performance. The most widespread frustration of local executives and legislators is their disappointment in agency performance. In an integrated system, budget allocations can be coupled with dated performance targets for program output, quality, efficiency, and effectiveness. Administrators know precisely what is expected of them and that the failure to satisfy those expectations will be a matter of concern to the chief executive and the legislature. This introduces a capacity for managerial and executive control that is all but absent in traditional government structures.

Lastly, an integrated financial management system will build up over time the hard information on program costs, performance, and effectiveness that, more often than not, is missing in local government today. Legislators and chief executives alike must frequently make spending decisions on the basis of sparse and unverified information on programs. They must deal with competing arguments on the merits of optional program activities, rarely supported by an independent evaluation of performance and results. Having the facts can make the job more manageable.

On balance, an integrated system is desirable both from the viewpoint of dollars and cents and from that of more responsive management. To get an idea of how far your community may have to go to achieve those benefits, look at the checklist in the next chapter.

A Checklist to Evaluate Local Financial Management 2

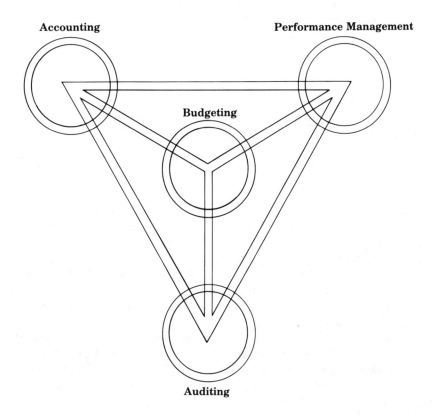

Accounting

Performance Management

Budgeting

Auditing

"Where does your community stand?"

A fully integrated financial management system must meet several demanding standards. First, the four component systems of budgeting, accounting, performance measurement, and auditing must be fully up to snuff. Second, the "linkages" that connect these basic fiscal systems must be taken into account.

This chapter contains a checklist to let you see how far your locality has advanced along the road to integration. The checklist is organized by financial management systems. The questions at the end of each section are those dealing with linkages between parts of the four systems.

Don't be surprised if you find that your community fails to score high on any one of the components—and especially if you can't in all honesty claim to have forged the linkages that ought to connect the basic systems. Few municipalities in the nation can claim to meet these standards today. What's more important is using the checklist to see how you stack up against a tough and demanding standard so that you can get a reasonable sense of the distance you have to travel.

How To Use This Checklist

This checklist can be used in a variety of ways. Its most basic use is to let you conduct a quick-and-dirty assessment of where your community stands on the road to a fully integrated system. There's no simple scoring method that will give you a "pass" or "fail" or grade your community's financial systems precisely. But every one of the questions should be able to be answered in the "yes" column. Every "no" that you enter in response to a question in the checklist is cause for concern and possible remediation. If you have to answer "no" to most of the questions in any part of the checklist, that is a pretty good indication of where your community has some distance to travel before its fiscal system can claim to be fully adequate and/or integrated.

If you can honestly answer "yes" to forty or more of the forty-seven questions, you probably don't need to go on reading this volume. In fact, you may find your municipality cited in this volume as one of the national leaders in the field.

On the other hand, if you get a score of twenty or less, your priority need is upgrading of your basic fiscal systems before you worry too much about system integration. Without a sound basic set of fiscal systems, movement toward integration may well obstruct your progress in meeting more fundamental requirements.

Most local governments will score above twenty and below forty. For example, a medium-size or larger city or county with a tradition of professional management should ordinarily have a score of thirty or more; usually, the "no" answers will reflect the lack of fully up-to-date accounting and performance management systems and the limitation of audit scope to financial and compliance matters.

You should also look at how your government scores in each of the four component lists. The following observations may help you.

- *Budget.* Most local governments should be able to answer at least eight of the twelve questions affirmatively. The three questions on budget analysis allow for partial coverage of the various kinds of analysis.
- *Budget Administration and Accounting.* Officials of some local jurisdictions may be surprised to find that they can answer "yes" to only four or five of the fourteen questions in this checklist. You will lose three to five points if you don't have a modern, multiple-classification accounting system, another three for not following GAAFR* standards, and as many as four for a poor structure for budget administration.
- *Performance Measurement.* There may be a sizable number of local governments which cannot provide an affirmative answer for any of the thirteen questions in this checklist. Where this is so, our scoring system has probably overrated the quality of the budget—since the substance of budget analysis depends so much on performance management. If your local government scores eight or more, it's almost certainly above average in this area.
- *Audit.* There are eight questions in this checklist. Most local governments will be able to answer "yes" to question 4.1 (that they do have an annual audit) and, often, to question 4.7 (that the audit assesses the accounting system and internal controls). Four more positive answers are possible with a well-managed program of financial and compliance audits. The last two require the use of performance or management audits.

Another way to use the checklist is as a guide to how familiar you are with your own locality's fiscal systems. Don't be disturbed if you aren't sure how your locality stacks up against sound practice. Few local government managers and legislators are really in a position to get a good overview of all the financial systems in their own government. We hope, however, that if this turns out to be your situation, we've whetted your appetite to get the answers. The succeeding chapters of this volume explain what's meant by each of the questions in the checklist—and why a "yes" response is important if you want your municipality to have a high quality, integrated financial management system.

---

*See chapter 6 for an explanation.

1. The Budget Checklist

1.1   *Comprehensive Budget Coverage.* Does the budget cover all of the funds expended by the local government?

         YES   NO

        ☐   ☐

1.2   *Budget Staff.* Is there a professional budget staff person or unit responsible to the chief executive that works for him in preparing the executive budget?

         YES   NO

        ☐   ☐

1.3   *Operating Budget: Revenues.* Is there an established procedure for developing and periodically updating estimates of revenue?

         YES   NO

        ☐   ☐

1.4   *Operating Budget: Expenditures by Program.* Is the operating budget formulated in terms of programs and activities (defined in terms of major purposes) rather than solely by organizational unit or objects of expenditure?

         YES   NO

        ☐   ☐

1.5   *Budget Analysis.* In the review of proposed agency budgets, does the budget staff person or unit:

- Analyze program costs per unit of workload or service delivered?

         YES   NO

        ☐   ☐

- Evaluate program benefits against costs?

         YES   NO

        ☐   ☐

● Estimate future year expenditures for proposed new programs and activities?

YES   NO

☐   ☐

1.6 *Capital Budget*. Is there a separate capital budget or separate capital component of a consolidated budget that lists individual capital projects and provides basic financial data on them?

YES   NO

☐   ☐

● Does the capital budget include estimates of the future impact of projects on the operating budget?

YES   NO

☐   ☐

1.7 *Multi-Year Fiscal Planning*. Does the executive budget include a multiyear financial plan that covers:

● The Operating Budget?

YES   NO

☐   ☐

● The Capital Budget?

YES   NO

☐   ☐

1.8 *Legislative Review*. Does the process leading up to the adoption of the budget(s) include examination of the executive budget by a fiscal staff person or unit responsible to the local legislature?

YES   NO

☐   ☐

2. The Budget Administration and Accounting Checklist

2.1 *Budget Allotments.* After the budget has been approved, is spending authority allotted by periodic intervals (e.g., quarterly) during the fiscal year so that agencies know their spending limits?

YES   NO
☐   ☐

2.2 *Responsibility Centers.* Are funds appropriated or allocated to the heads of organizational units so that financial and managerial authority is clearly integrated?

YES   NO
☐   ☐

2.3 *Budget Modification.* Are agency heads or program managers authorized to reallocate funds within program appropriations (without coming back to the chief executive, budget staff, or legislative body for each change)?

YES   NO
☐   ☐

2.4 *Budget Control.* Are there periodic reports to the chief executive and local legislature on actual expenditures, encumbrances, and revenues against the adopted budget plan?

YES   NO
☐   ☐

2.5 *Accounting Basis.* Does the accounting system operate on an accrual basis (modified as appropriate and approved under GAAFR) for both revenues and expenditures?

YES   NO
☐   ☐

2.6 *Municipal Enterprises.* Does the municipality have full accrual accounting for its independent revenue-supported enterprises?

YES   NO
☐   ☐

2.7   *Internal Controls.* Are there written accounting procedures that clearly set forth a system of internal controls?

YES ☐   NO ☐

2.8   *Accounting Schedule.* Are the financial reports of the government certified by the Municipal Finance Officers Association?

YES ☐   NO ☐

2.9   *Flexible Account Structure.* Does the accounting system have the capacity to provide data on expenditures and encumbrances not merely for each appropriation but also for—

- Program elements and activities used in budget analysis and presentation?

YES ☐   NO ☐

- Projects financed under special grants?

YES ☐   NO ☐

- Major organizational divisions?

YES ☐   NO ☐

- Major geographic divisions of the locality?

YES ☐   NO ☐

2.10   *Common Data Base.* Does the accounting system produce data on expenditures and encumbrances for the programs, activities, and projects for which performance measurement data are collected?

YES ☐   NO ☐

2.11 *Cost Accounting.* Is there a capacity to generate the data required to determine the full costs of individual programs, activities, and special projects?

YES   NO

☐   ☐

3. Performance Management Checklist

3.1 *Central System.* Does the locality have a performance management system covering the activities of all or most of its operating agencies?

YES   NO

☐   ☐

3.2 *Component Systems.* If there is not a comprehensive system, is there a system that covers one or more individual agencies?

YES   NO

☐   ☐

3.3 *Contents of System.* Does the performance management system contain the following items:

- Measures or indicators of workload for relevant programs, activities, and projects?

YES   NO

☐   ☐

- Measures or indicators of output for relevant programs, activities, or projects?

YES   NO

☐   ☐

- Measures or indicators of effectiveness or quality of performance?

YES   NO

☐   ☐

3.4   *Management Plan.* Is there a regularly produced plan that sets forth the performance/productivity targets on an annual or more frequent basis?

YES   NO

☐   ☐

3.5   *Performance Reporting.* Is there periodic reporting on progress against the targets set in the annual performance plan?

YES   NO

☐   ☐

• To the chief executive?

YES   NO

☐   ☐

• To the public?

YES   NO

☐   ☐

3.6   *Management Projects and Assistance.* Is there a staff assigned to help local agencies undertake special improvement projects and activities?

YES   NO

☐   ☐

3.7   *Executive Management Participation.* Does the chief executive play an active part in reviewing the results of the performance/productivity program and in requiring agency adherence to targets?

YES   NO

☐   ☐

3.8   *Linkages to Budgeting.* Is the performance management system integrated with the budget process?

• Are performance data systematically used in budget analysis and reported with expenditure data in the budget?

YES   NO

☐   ☐

- Are performance targets and objectives related to recommended appropriations included in the budget?

YES   NO

☐   ☐

4. Audit Checklist

4.1 *Periodic Audit.* Is the municipal accounting system and its records and procedures audited annually by an independent public accountant?

YES   NO

☐   ☐

4.2 *Financial Audit.* In addition to the annual independent audit, does the local government retain qualified auditors (on a staff or consulting basis) to conduct periodic in-depth reviews of the financial operations of selected municipal activities?

YES   NO

☐   ☐

4.3 *Performance or Management Audits.* Does the municipality have a continuing program of audits (operated on a staff or consulting basis) of the economy and efficiency of performance and the results achieved in selected municipal activities?

YES   NO

☐   ☐

4.4 *Audit Response.* Has a standard procedure been established for responding to financial and performance audits to insure that there is adequate feedback into the budgetary process?

YES   NO

☐   ☐

4.5 *Audit Planning.* Is a statement specifying scope and coverage prepared in advance of each audit?

YES   NO

☐   ☐

4.6   *Budget Involvement.* Does the budget staff participate in planning or by proposing subjects for inclusion in the program of selected financial and/or performance audits?

YES   NO

☐   ☐

4.7   *Accounting System Audit.* Does the annual independent audit provide for an appraisal and assessment of the adequacy of the municipality's accounting system and the related internal controls?

YES   NO

☐   ☐

4.8   *Performance Audit.* Is there a program for the periodic or selected audit of the performance management program?

YES   NO

☐   ☐

Budgeting: The Local Government's Planning Tool 3

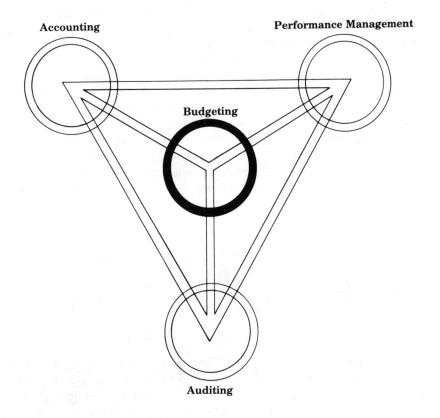

Accounting

Performance Management

Budgeting

Auditing

"proposal and disposal"

Budgeting is the process of allocating a locality's scarcest resource—the funds available to support local activities—among a host of competing demands.

The budget is a central element in decision making—if, indeed, it is not the central element. The budget is the locality's plan for how it will allocate its resources to meet the most pressing requirements for personnel, equipment, and facilities. While there are other important decisions that face the executive and legislative leadership of a locality, there is little question that virtually all governmental decisions are at least conditioned and constrained by the harsh realities of the budget. This fact of public life is true at all times, but it has come to the fore with unusual force at the present time because of the continuing pressures of inflation and tax revolt that create today's reality in most local governments.

American communities vary over an extraordinary range in terms of population size, density of development, and form of government. "Strong mayor" cities, management by commission, city, county, or town managers, and governance by town meeting—even these cover only a fraction of the constellation of approaches to how cities, towns, villages, counties, boroughs, and other local jurisdictions are governed. But nearly every locality goes through a process of preparing and adopting a budget as a principal step in its annual decision-making cycle.

No other activity in which municipal managers and legislators engage occupies a more important role than budgeting. Virtually every public action requires some commitment of municipal funds. These commitments can only be obtained through one or another aspect of the budget process.

The discussion in this chapter covers four principal topics:

- The key aspects of local budgeting
- The different local budgets
- Balancing the budget: The rules of the game
- The budget process

Key Aspects of Local Budgeting

Before we proceed to look at the different types of local budget, it may help to set a framework if we consider some of the key aspects of the budget process. The next sections discuss the executive budget concept, the principal "players" in the budget process and its three key aspects.

The Executive Budget

In most local and state governments in the United States, the annual budget is initially prepared as a single, unified document by the chief executive who then submits it for review, change, and approval by the legislature. The movement toward this approach was led by the federal government in the trail-blazing Budget and Accounting Act of 1921.

In the earliest patterns, local budgets were formulated by legislators who considered many separate requests and tried to negotiate them into some semblance of equitable arrangement as they adopted appropriations and made decisions on how to raise the necessary funds. Instead of a unified budget, this process tended to produce a series of often poorly related appropriation acts. The concept of the executive budget arose as a result of growing unease over budgeting when legislative bodies responded directly to the competing demands of numerous agencies, boards, and commissions.

Demand for an executive budget process became one of the central rallying points of the municipal reform movement in the first quarter of this century. Generally, what was sought and won by the reformers was the assignment of the task of budget formulation to the chief executive. It was to be the task of the executive to consider the competing demands for local resources and to assemble them into a balanced program for consideration by the legislature. The budgetary responsibility of the executive was to propose and that of the legislature to dispose—by changing or confirming the budgetary initiatives of the executive. The departments and other operating units of government were responsible for administering the adopted budget within the legal limits set by the legislature.

Of course, one must speak of a uniform approach to budgeting with some caution in a nation with fifty state governments, over 3000 counties, and upwards of 75,000 independent or quasi-independent units of local government. And yet if there is any unifying theme at all within this vast array of difference, it is the degree to which this pattern of executive budget formulation, legislative adoption, and executive administration holds true today from Maine to Hawaii.

Players in the Budgetary Game

The important role that budgeting occupies in local public management has meant that there are many forces that seek to influence its outcome. At some point, virtually every resident and organization concerned with public service or taxes is affected by the budget. In turn, they seek to influence its formation and contents.

It's not possible, within the limits of this guide, to examine the role of every participant in the budgetary "game," but we should at least look at the roles of the principal players. They include the following:

- *The chief executive* has the principal responsibility for budget formulation (putting the proposed budget together in a single document). He or she retains the ultimate responsibility for seeing that the budgetary plan, once accepted by the legislature, is adhered to by all the other agencies of government. In many localities, the chief executive is elected; in many others he or she is an appointed manager. In some cases, there is even a "plural" executive, composed of several selectmen or commissioners.

- *The legislature* may be a city or county council, a county or legislature, a board of selectmen, alderman, or supervisors. It is almost always elected by the voters. Its principal budgetary responsibilities are the decisions on what revenues to raise and what expenditures to allow. The legislature also has a vital "oversight" responsibility in assessing the performance of the operating agencies that comprise the branches of government as they carry out their budgetary assignments.

Implied or required by the roles of these two principal players in the budgetary game are roles assigned to significant supporting players. They include the following:

- *The central budget agency* assists the executive in budget formation and administration. This unit can range in size from a single part-time fiscal aide to a budget staff of hundreds of trained examiners and analysts. It can be an independent staff unit within the office of the chief executive or can operate as a component of a larger department whose responsibilities include general administration, revenue collection, accounting or personal functions.
- *The operating agencies* are the units of government which actually carry out the delivery of public services within the guidelines of the fiscal plan set forth in the budget. Typically, those operating agencies also have their own internal budget staffs.

Other public agencies that play roles in or related to the budget process include "overhead" units such as personnel management (administration of civil service regulations, collective bargaining, and other aspects of the personnel function); revenue collection agencies; accounting, auditing and other fiscal control units; and agencies that monitor municipal management practices.

In addition, nonpublic organizations and groups often play important parts in the budgetary process. Among the types of private organization that are often involved in local budgeting are citizen budget or fiscal research commissions; public interest groups of a wide variety of kinds; business associations; unions; religious groups; and many neighborhood or civic associations. These organizations actively propose or oppose items of expenditure or revenue. They may be involved in trying to influence the process of budget formulation or administration but most often they tend to concentrate their efforts on the most visible act in the process—budget adoption.

Three Key Functions of Budgeting

In order to understand more fully the role of budgeting, it is useful to divide it into three different functional aspects, each one of which corresponds to a vital feature of local governance. The three aspects are control, management, and planning.*

Control. Budgeting would be meaningless if expenditures were not controlled to accord with budget limitations. There must be some assurance that funds are expended only for the purposes for which they were appropriated, that spending is limited to the amounts appropriated, and that appropriations for continuing functions are not exhausted prior to the completion of the period they were intended to cover.

In fact, the origins of American municipal budgeting in the nineteenth century are connected with patterns of corruption and improper spending that characterized many of the big cities in that era. A fundamental requirement of public budgeting became the need to assure that appropriations were being spent for the purpose intended by the legislature in its approval of the budget. In its simplest sense, this requirement meant that if money was appropriated for a teacher's salary or to buy a police car, then that was what it was to be used for. A parallel meaning was that no expenditure was to be made unless there was an appropriation for it.

The introduction of the control concept as the basis of the budget process led to what was described as the "line-item" approach to budgeting. Each proposed item of expenditure was to be listed in as much detail as possible so that a careful record could be maintained to control spending and limit it to legitimate items. Budgets became detailed lists of proposed items of expenditure with each public employee's salary and each item of supply or equipment listed separately so that as spending occurred it could be checked off against an appropriation line.

The "line-item" budget, together with other municipal reforms such as the introduction of civil service and competitive bidding on provision of services or supplies led to a great improvement in control. A less desirable accompaniment of this detailed approach to budgeting was a parallel increase in the bureaucratic procedures necessary to check on spending. Agencies were required to keep detailed records and, in addi-

---

*The first statement of these three vital aspects of budgeting of which we are aware was in a seminal article on budgeting by Alan Schick: "The Road to PPB," in *Public Administration Review* (December 1966).

tion, were often required to obtain central budget agency approval before making even the most minute change in their lists of line items. In many cases, they were even required to obtain legislative approval to make changes (e.g., to fill a position when even a few dollars of difference arose between the previously approved salary and what was actually to be paid). Where the local government's operations were simple and involved few agencies and few types of position and when the pace of change was slow, this expansion of procedure could be accommodated without too great difficulty. On the other hand, where these conditions didn't hold true— as for example in larger cities or rapidly growing suburbs—the result of the "line-item" approach was to bury budget agencies and legislatures under a vast array of minute change actions to modify the initial appropriation schedule. At the same time, virtually all attention became focused on the details of expenditure rather than on its basic purpose—the efficient provision of public services.

Management.   Once the effort to control the details of public expenditure had succeeded, the attention of people concerned with improving local government began to shift to issues of performance. Improved management in the public sector was sought to achieve in public service delivery some of the same efficiency that had been demonstrated by private corporations.

Performance budgeting embodies the management-oriented approach to the budget. Schick described the principal thrust of performance budgeting as

> to help administrators to assess the work-efficiency of operating units by (1) casting budget categories in functional terms, and (2) providing work-cost measurements to facilitate the efficient performance of prescribed activities.

The management orientation, in its purest form, left policy making to others. General Dawes, one of the early directors of the federal Bureau of the Budget, once explained that if Congress decided that all of the garbage in the District of Columbia was to be piled on the White House steps, the function of the Bureau of the Budget was merely to determine how this might be most efficiently done.

One concern of the thrust toward improved efficiency focused on the performance of governmental staffs and units. At its most detailed level, it was concerned with the number of items of activity performed by each public employee; for example, how many letters were typed per typist, how many permits were processed per clerk, how many calls were responded to per policeman.

This detailed approach has limited value because, for the most part, government services aren't provided by individuals acting alone but rather by units or organizations. For example, the policeman responds to calls after being notified by a central communication unit and is supported by a variety of other staff units. The fire department dispatches teams of firemen and usually more than one vehicle to a single response. Pages typed per secretary provide data more relevant to personal evaluation than to whether the unit in which the secretary works is performing competently.

For these reasons, the primary focus of the performance budget was on the efficiency with which operations were carried out by the various work units responsible for their execution. The work of the government was seen in terms of activities and tasks and of the organizational units performing them.

The administration of the control-oriented budget was, for obvious reasons, a job for accountants and during the primacy of the control objective, budget bureaus tended to be staffed by accountants. The management-oriented budget, on the other hand, called for management experts, industrial engineers, and efficiency experts.

Planning.   The planning approach to budgeting emphasizes neither fiscal control nor operational efficiency but, rather, the rational resolution of policy choices in both expenditure and revenue raising. Schick, in this connection, quotes Robert Anthony's definition of strategic planning as

> the process of deciding on objectives of the organization, on changes in these objectives, on the resources used to attain these objectives, and the policies that are to govern the acquisition, use and disposition of these resources.

Whereas a management-oriented approach to, say, a manpower training program would aim at maximizing the efficiency and, perhaps, the effectiveness of its operation, a planning approach would stress broader issues, such as whether the program were actually needed, whether the job might be better done through changes in school programs or by employer-administered on-the-job training, and whether the program's benefits in relation to its cost warranted its continuation in preference to either some other spending proposal or to a tax reduction.

The planning approach to budgeting has several important characteristics:

- Government operations are perceived primarily in terms of their purposes or objectives.
- The budget is organized by programs defined by the objectives they serve rather than by object or activity.
- The emphasis is upon budget decision making rather than on budget administration.

- Program choices are made on the basis of relative cost-effectiveness in comparison with alternative means of achieving the same objective.
- Multiyear planning is an explicit part of the process—a recognition of the limitations of the one-year budget and the longer term impact of current budget decisions.
- The skills and perspectives of economists, systems analysts, and planners are stressed.

Philosophically, the planning approach is a marked departure from the management-oriented budget. In practice, however, there are areas of overlap. The broad purpose-defined programs of the planning-oriented budget can be subdivided into the activities and tasks of the management budget. Program analysis for the planning-oriented budget must also contend with the issues of operational efficiency with which the management-oriented budget is primarily concerned. Similarly, performance analysis will, in some cases, enter the broader area of cost-effectiveness analysis. Both demand extensive budget analysis.

Three Functions in a Single Budget

A modern budget system must serve all three purposes: control, management, and planning. This, as many local governments have learned, is not easy. A different organization of budgetary information is required for each purpose. Each purpose further involves a markedly different perspective on the budget process and depends upon different methods and techniques. Difficult as it is, there are a substantial number of local governments that have developed budget systems that effectively serve all three functions.

The evolution of budgeting from the expenditure control function to eventually embrace all three purposes has involved a progressive increase in the complexity and magnitude of the demands placed by budgeting on the other three financial management processes: accounting, auditing, and performance management.

- Accounting and budgeting were most compatible and most effectively interrelated when both shared a dominant orientation toward expenditure control. With the extension of budget responsibilities for management and planning, budgeting has come to require accounting information on costs as well as expenditures and on a myriad of additional categories—programs, subprograms, activities, tasks, and organizational units.
- Similarly, the financial compliance audit and an auditor's opinion of the government's financial statements would satisfy a control-

oriented budget. Today, there is an increasing need for broader evaluations of program efficiency and effectiveness.

- Performance management could provide a useful but limited function in providing data on work or output per unit of manpower without any close connection with financial management save for the use of the data in budget analysis. The broader budget concepts require a richer diet of effectiveness data and information on relevant community conditions as well as integration with the accounting data needed for cost analysis.

The reader of this volume will, consequently, find that the need for more effective integration of financial management functions is, in large part, directly related to the development of the current broad concept of the budget function.

The planning approach to public budgeting was given a major boost in the early 1960s when a planning-programming-budgeting system (PPBS) was introduced in the Defense Department. President Lyndon B. Johnson, impressed with the additional information and options for executive decision the new system offered, ordered its adoption in 1965 by all federal agencies. Many state and local governments followed suit.

Long before the advent of PPBS, both advance planning and cost-benefit analysis were employed, to some extent, in the budget process for capital investments (such as water supply and pollution control facilities). An even more recent development, still in its early stages in even the most advanced municipalities, is the extension of the planning concept to the operating budget which finances current activities. Some—but not very many—localities now prepare two- or three-year forecasts of their operating budgets.

The Local Budgets

Localities put their budgets together in many different ways. In this part, we'll talk about the budget primarily in terms of the two different types of budget with which most municipal officials are familiar: operating and capital. Typically, the operating budget pays for annually recurring expenses, such as salaries of public employees, supplies, and rent on buildings used but not owned by the municipality. The capital budget pays for the cost of constructing buildings and purchasing major pieces of equipment such as trucks. Almost all localities maintain their operating budgets in consolidated, published form; many do the same with their capital budgets but some smaller localities never produce a formal capital budget document, preferring to treat each capital expenditure as a separate and distinct activity.

In the subsequent sections, we will divide the municipal budgets somewhat more precisely. First, the operating budget will be discussed in terms of its two separate components: revenues and expenditures. Under capital budgeting we will consider not only the annual budget but also the capital plan (or programs) for succeeding years; this is important because many capital projects take several years to complete, and it is essential to plan for subsequent year requirements when the initial budgetary commitment is made. We will also examine some other aspects of local resource allocation which have many of the characteristics of budgets, such as the Community Development Block Grant. These extra "budgets" are very important aspects of local management and resource allocation in many communities.

In this discussion we won't be trying to tell the reader all about each of the local budgets. To do so would require a much longer volume than this—but if you want more details on the budget process than you find here, the Bibliography in the back of this book lists many of the best publications on public budgeting.

What we will try to do is to focus most directly on the information needed to do competent budgeting. It is these information requirements that underlie the most important relationships among budgeting, accounting, performance management, and auditing.

The Operating Budget: Revenues

Money is what budgeting is all about. And the common experience of most American communities is that most years there just isn't enough to go around. As a result, revenues tend to be the dominant feature of local budgeting.

It is critical to an understanding of municipal budgeting that the concept of balance between revenue resources and the public services and facilities that the resources must pay for be kept in mind. It is this feature of budgeting that disciplines the entire process.

At one time, the real property tax—one of the most stable and predictable revenue sources—accounted for the lion's share of the revenues of local government. The budgeting and collection of revenue was, under these circumstances, a relatively simple matter. As exhibit 3-1 shows, the real property tax still accounts for 30 percent of all local government revenue. State aid and locally raised revenues other than property tax receipts each now account for about the same proportion of local revenues as the property tax; the balance is provided largely through federal aid. Among local governments, municipalities are the least dependent upon property taxes and state aid. The exhibit shows a wide diversity among the different types of local governments in source of revenues. The differences are even more pronounced from state to state and among individual jurisdictions. Yet, the vast majority of American local governments

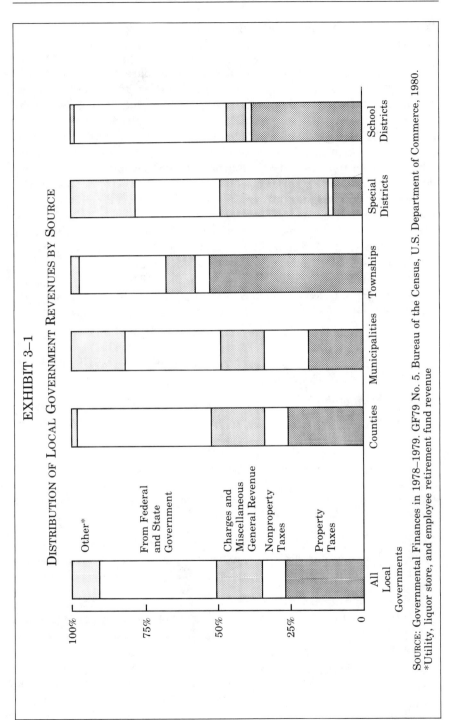

EXHIBIT 3–1

DISTRIBUTION OF LOCAL GOVERNMENT REVENUES BY SOURCE

Other*

From Federal
and State
Government

Charges and
Miscellaneous
General Revenue

Nonproperty
Taxes

Property
Taxes

All
Local
Governments

Counties

Municipalities

Townships

Special
Districts

School
Districts

100%

75%

50%

25%

0

SOURCE: Governmental Finances in 1978–1979. GF79 No. 5. Bureau of the Census, U.S. Department of Commerce, 1980.
*Utility, liquor store, and employee retirement fund revenue

face, albeit in varying degrees, the same general problems in budgeting revenues. The following are the most important of those problems.

Limited Local Authority Over Revenues. The representative local government depends upon federal and state aid for 39 percent of all its revenue. For the average school district, grants-in-aid finance nearly half the budget. The amount of aid received by any locality may be increased modestly by aggressive efforts to obtain certain grants but, in the main, aid depends upon grant distribution formulae in state and federal legislation. Federal and state contributions to local revenue, hence, can and do change in accord with action to continue, terminate, or modify programs. At various times during the 1970s, local governments faced cutbacks in grant funds as the Congress and state legislatures responded to budgetary pressures. The extent, if any, to which grants would be increased to cover inflationary increases in needs has, in addition, been a continuing source of uncertainty in local government.

Local control over locally raised revenues is far from complete. In many states, property taxes are subject to limits imposed by state law or constitutions. Nonproperty taxes are often similarly limited to specified maximum rates. For localities with tax rates at or near the limits, this has either resulted in sometimes frantic efforts to find other revenue sources or shifted the focus of revenue raising to persuading the state legislature to modify existing tax limits.

Reduced Predictability of Revenues. The increased reliance on grants-in-aid has, as the discussion suggests, reduced not merely local control over revenues, but also the extent to which revenues could be accurately estimated and budgeted. Reduced predictability has also resulted from the rising use of sales, income, and other nonproperty taxes which now account for nearly one-tenth of all local government revenue. Revenue from these taxes is more sensitive to changes in economic conditions than property tax revenue.

Limitations on the Use of Revenue. A very large proportion of local revenue is restricted for certain specified purposes and cannot be used to meet the general revenue needs of the local government.

- Except for general revenue sharing and some comparable state aid programs, grants-in-aid are provided only for specified programs and projects and must be spent in accord with detailed grantor requirements.
- Utility system revenue on a nationwide basis only marginally exceeds the cost of utility system operation. A few local governments receive substantial surpluses from utility operations but most do not.

- Retirement system contributions must be held in trust for the pensions of the contributing employees.
- User charges are often limited to finance the services for which they were levied—and even some taxes are earmarked for particular purposes.
- Special assessments must be used to finance the special improvements for which they were received.

These limitations mean that, in important respects, local governments must budget revenues for a whole set of different budgets rather than a single comprehensive budget. Indeed, some of the revenues are so restricted as to require the establishment of separate funds to assure that revenues are not diverted to other purposes.

Another significant limitation is local spending that applies in many states come in the form of "caps" or upper limits on local taxation. These limits may be set by state law or in the constitution and can apply to the total amount of taxes that can be raised and/or to the rate of increase in local tax rates. For example, a recent referendum in Massachusetts set an upper limit of 2½ percent on local real estate taxes (as a fraction of property values) and also restrained tax rate gains to no more than 2½ percent per year.

The Operating Budget: Expenditures

The pressures of many demands for public service, coupled with inflationary price increases that make the cost of just maintaining the same services higher each year, are what makes local budgeting difficult. The severe limitations on fund raising mean that most municipal budgeting is "revenue-driven" in the words of Aaron Wildavsky, a noted scholarly observer of public budget practices.

Nevertheless, what most people think of when they think of budgeting is what the budget will buy in the way of refuse collection, police protection, recreation services, and other desirable municipal activities. These expenditures constitute the "good" side of the budget in contrast to the unpleasant but essential requirements of tax collection.

The expenditure side of the operating budget is made up of many different items that can be viewed in many different ways. In most localities, what's included in the operating budget are all recurring expenditures (salaries are a typical and major example) and all expenditures for items that have a short life-span (such as supplies or small items of equipment). There isn't any absolute rule, however. In many cases, state law or state comptroller rulings define what must be paid for out of the annual operating budget, but there are always some items which fall at the edges of the definition. Automobiles and trucks are an example of two relatively similar items, both of which are sometimes required to be included in the operating budget. At other times and places, autos are in the operating budget and trucks in the capital budget. And in some cases both can fall in the capital budget.

In general, localities are allowed (but not required) to put *any* legitimate expenditure into their operating budgets. In some localities, even capital facilities are financed on a "pay as you go" basis out of the operating budget.

There are four basic ways in which budgeting looks at the expenditure items that make up the operating budget:

- *Object Classification.* Every item falls into some "object" classification depending on its nature. Personnel costs such as salaries and fringe benefits make up one group of objects of expenditure. Other common objects of expenditure include supplies, rent, heat and light, and telephone costs.
- *Organizational Classification.* A basic way of grouping expenditures is by the municipal agency responsible for them. In many cases, subunits such as divisions are important enough for separate identification in the budget.
- *Program (or Functional) Classification.* Every item of expenditure also falls into one or more categories which describe its use or purpose. For example, the group of municipal employees engaged in criminal justice activities—plus all the costs associated with them (salaries, fringe benefits, supplies, etc.)—constitute a functional category even if the category includes more than just the police department by extending to such functions as those of the courts, district attorneys, correction department, etc.
- *Activity Classification.* Expenditures can also be grouped by the activity or operation performed such as street cleaning, tax collection, or police patrol. Activities may be used as a subclassification when the budget is classified by either organization or program.

The different ways in which budgets are classified are related to the three functions served by budgeting. *Control* is facilitated by the clear lines of responsibility of the organizational budget and by subdivision into objects of expenditure or line items. *Management* is aided by division into activities and tasks for which performance standards can be developed. *Planning*, on the other hand, needs a budget organized by function or program.

These different expenditure classification schemes have long been seen as alternatives. In fact, all of them are needed if the budget is to satisfy all three of its basic purposes.

The Capital Budget and Program

Most local governments budget separately for the purchase of land, major physical facilities and heavy equipment. This is a general pattern of separate appropriation for capital items covered by the operating budget, and it is therefore reasonable to expect capital facilities to be paid for over a longer time period.

Local revenues to pay for capital budget expenditures are usually derived from the sale of long-term bonds. Repayment periods usually range from five to forty years. In most cases, the annual debt service payments needed to cover the cost of interest and repayment of principal (amortization) are appropriated in the operating budget.

Some inherent characteristics of capital facilities have become reflected in the ways that local governments budget for them:

- Most capital projects not only involve substantial expenditures but take several years to complete. The purchase of a site or signing of an architectural contract implies greater expenditures in subsequent years for construction, equipment, and furnishing.
- Most localities have the capacity to finance only a limited number of capital projects in a given year. For example, the community may be able to budget for street or sewer construction in only one or two neighborhoods in a given year, even though it recognizes that other neighborhoods have needs that are almost as pressing.
- The capital budget tends to be an important element in the locality's long-range planning and development program. Its future year implications are critical to such factors as future operating expenses and patterns of community growth and change.

Each of these characteristics of capital projects tends to require multiyear thinking about the capital budget to a greater degree than most local officials feel is required, or even possible, with respect to the operating budget. The important role played in capital budgeting by multiyear planning usually results in the preparation of both a single-year capital budget and a multiyear capital program for the succeeding three to six years. The multiyear capital program itself should be closely linked to the locality's physical master plan in order to insure that capital projects and community development are properly integrated.

The accompanying illustration (exhibit 3–2) shows how the concept of the multiyear capital program grows naturally out of the nature of capital projects. The top half of the illustration shows in line diagram form the sequence of major activities for three typical capital projects: an elementary school, a police precinct house, and construction of a new street. The sequence of steps is important not only in time terms, but also in bud-

EXHIBIT 3–2

ILLUSTRATIVE EXAMPLE OF CAPITAL BUDGET AND FIVE-YEAR PROGRAM

Capital Budget				Capital Program		
Year	**1**	**2**	**3**	**4**	**5**	**6**
School	$500,000	$150,000		$3,000,000		$500,000
Police Station		100,000	$ 50,000	1,000,000		200,000
Highway			75,000		$2,000,000	
Total	500,000	250,000	125,000	4,000,000	2,000,000	700,000

Recapitulation: Capital Budget   (year 1) $ 500,000
                         Capital Program (years 2–6)   7,075,000

getary terms; it's likely that funds will be needed at each of these points to enable the project to move forward. Of course, all of the funds could be appropriated at the outset but this could cost the locality more if it actually borrowed the whole amount at the outset. The lower half of the diagram shows how each of the steps translates into a budgetary item in either the capital budget or in one of the succeeding years of the capital program.

This is a simple illustration of a three-item capital budget and program but it begins to suggest some of the important factors involved in the process. First, it shows the importance of the relationship between time and funding requirements. If progress on any one of the capital projects slips, it will not only delay the day when the community can benefit from the project, but it will also change financing plans. Secondly, the illustration shows clearly the "lumpiness" of capital appropriations. Even when the cost of each project is divided into subcomponents (site purchase, design contract, etc.) there is a tendency for major funding needs to be concentrated in one or another year. Notice, for example, how year 4 of the capital program calls for more than half of the total funds for all three projects in a single year. This might not be important in some localities where each project is considered as a separate item, not connected in any way to the others. But in most localities, if the first draft of the capital budget and program looked like the illustration, the chief executive and his budget staff would begin planning to see if they couldn't even out the expenditure pattern so that their financing plans looked better when they talked with their investment advisers about their bond issuance schedule.

Timing is a critical dimension in capital budgeting—if, indeed, it is not *the* critical dimension. In part, this is true for the reasons noted. It's also true because of two other features of capital construction. First, it's a complex process in which many things need to be carefully coordinated and where something always seems to go wrong (shortages of critical materials, strikes, unforeseen site clearance problems and a host of others). It's far more common to have projects take more time than to beat their target dates. Secondly, time is money in a very real sense in the construction business. Almost nowhere else in our economy has inflation had such dire effects. Also, perhaps in no other part of the budget process is the problem of forecasting more difficult; however hard engineers and architects try, they always seem to underestimate what construction costs will really turn out to be.

The vital connection between capital budgeting and timing has led to the development of management techniques that can give budgeters and construction managers more effective planning and control tools. These are discussed in chapter 7.

The financing of capital improvements is of great importance to the long-range fiscal health of the local government. In most localities, the capital budget is financed in the main through the issuance of serial bonds with maturities such that annual debt services—including both interest and debt amortization—remains the same each year over the life of the bond issue. The longest maturity should, for obvious reasons, not exceed the expected useful life of the improvement, and, often, maximum maturities for different types of capital facilities are specified by state law.

The planning of capital financing must take into account the effects of state limitations on local government debt which are usually set at a percentage of the real property tax base and of future ability to pay. Probable future capital needs must be considered and leeway left for their financing. Estimates must be made of the probable interest rate and, in some circumstances, of the marketability of the bonds.

Bonds may be general obligations supported by the full faith and credit of the local government or they may be revenue or other special bonds supported only by revenues earned by the improvement or dedicated to its financing. Usually, general obligation bonds pay lower interest rates than do revenue bonds, although many localities prefer to use revenue bonds where possible—among other reasons, because they normally don't require approval by a referendum of the voters.

Part of the costs of a capital project may be paid from federal or state aid or local government appropriations. Interim financing through bond anticipation notes will be necessary if a decision is made to issue bonds late in the project development period. On the other hand, if bonds are sold prior to development, the proceeds can be invested to cover the carrying costs of the funds until they are needed.

Decisions on capital financing are complex because they involve estimates or projections of likely future developments and because external judgments of local financial conditions will be heavily based upon the magnitude of debt and the quality of its management.

The "Other" Local Budgets

Most localities have other budgets in addition to their operating and capital budgets. These other budgets—often not called or even recognized as such—may be important components of the local fiscal scene. Some of these other local budgets arise as a result of federal aid programs which are not fully integrated into either the operating or capital budget. Others arise out of special financing arrangements whereby fees or even some taxes are paid directly to municipal agencies and are dedicated to the support of particular services. Water and sewer systems are often operated in this way; some communities operate electric generating and distribution systems; others operate low and moderate income housing programs.

Many localities are eligible for federal funds under the Community Development Block Grant (CDBG) Program which provides funds that can be used for both capital and operating purposes to assist low and moderate income families. CDBG funds are often provided and must be accounted for on a different fiscal year than local funds. They can also be used for some purposes and in ways that aren't easy to fit into the structure of either the local operating or capital budgets (for example, loans or advances to nonprofit housing corporations). As a result, many localities have found it more convenient to maintain a separate CDBG budget. While the separate CDBG budget may provide some convenience for local operations, it's important that it be closely linked to the locality's other budgets because CDBG funds can often finance projects and activities that otherwise would have to be paid for out of the local operating or capital budget.

The same need for linkage arises with respect to yet other local budgets. For example, many localities have independent or quasiindependent housing, urban renewal or economic development authorities that maintain their own budgets but that in many cases obtain part of their funds from the local government. Public transportation agencies often follow something of the same pattern of substantial but not complete fiscal independence from the local budget. Similar patterns of independence exist with respect to water and sewer agencies and park agencies in some localities—although in most places they are regular government departments. Perhaps most important of all, in terms of impact on the local tax base, school boards are often independent in administration and financing from the general governments that serve the same jurisdiction.

A variety of special districts also complicate the fiscal patterns of many localities. County governments provide most local services in many parts of the nation; in other places they are responsible for only a few services (or, as in Connecticut, none at all).

Our purpose here is not to criticize the often complex fiscal arrangements by which local government functions are provided in the United States. Indeed, this diversity may well be one of the strengths of local government, enabling it to adapt to particular situations and to avoid painful confrontations over what level of government should provide which service or control which fiscal resources. On the other hand, it is clear that this complex pattern does raise difficulties for local executives and budget staffs as they seek to build information systems that will enable them to anticipate and track the fiscal consequences of their own budget decisions. Some of the unfortunate consequences of governmental complexity can be readily cited:

- Poor fiscal planning or operation by quasiindependent public agencies can have damaging impact on general government, either by impairing the fiscal reputation of an otherwise carefully managed locality or by sudden demands for subsidies.
- In other cases, the opposite situation can occur. An independent authority or special district can preempt valuable fiscal resources and operate in relative wealth while the general governments in the same jurisdiction face severe hardships in raising funds for basic services. Transportation authorities which capture the revenues from bridge or tunnel tolls are among the instances of such wealthy operations; you can tell where their jurisdiction ends as the pavement becomes pot-holed and uneven.

In terms of the focus of this guide—the development of integrated financial systems—these separate jurisdiction situations present a challenging task to which, at best, only partial answers can be suggested at the present time. An initial key to dealing with the issue is to increase awareness and information flow among the governmental entities involved. To the degree that common fiscal principles can be followed in such matters as budgeting practices and accounting standards, the situation can also be eased.

Balancing the Budget: The Rules of the Game

In the 1970s, for the first time since the great depression, a number of major local governments had serious financial emergencies resulting in default on debt repayment, deferred payrolls, and/or delayed payments to suppliers. The emergencies resulted in disclosures of deep-rooted problems that had been hidden or understated through years of nominally balanced budgets.

The experience underlined, especially for the municipal security markets, the fact that the significance of a balanced budget or of a deficit or surplus depends upon the budgetary and accounting practices followed by the reporting government.

There are a number of practices that can undermine the integrity and viability of the budget and/or contribute to longer run fiscal problems. They are not difficult to identify. They include

- *Overestimating revenues.* This is, perhaps, the most common budgetary problem. Deliberate inflation of revenue projections is probably less common than genuine but unwarranted optimism and the failure to fully reflect likely changes in economic conditions. Conservative revenue estimation is the only safe course unless the locality has an adequate reserve fund or has included a reserve against contingencies in the budget totals.

- *Underestimating expenditures.* Unforeseen events such as recession and inflation can cause expenditure problems in virtually any locality. So can events such as cutbacks in state or federal aid. But, expenditures are sometimes deliberately underestimated or major incremental factors (such as collective bargaining costs) may not be included in the budget plan. The cure is much the same as for overestimated revenue—adequate reserves.
- *Underfinancing of pension and other obligations.* Some local governments do not fund employee retirement systems on an actuarial basis, paying instead only the current bill for benefit payments. This practice shifts current costs to future years. The most common corrective action is a long-term program for a gradual increase in contributions aimed at eventually meeting actuarial standards.

  Other unfunded liabilities often include the "banks" of unutilized sick leave and vacation days owed to local employees as well as other severance pay obligations.
- *Cash accounting.* Those local governments charging expenditures only when actually disbursed tend to be vulnerable to unforeseen changes in the economic environment. Control over spending cannot be fully effective without control at the point of obligation or commitment.
- *Short-term borrowing.* Some local governments borrow seasonally in anticipation of revenues due later in the fiscal year, and some follow a regular practice of borrowing against revenues earned but not yet received. Even soundly based short-term borrowing will expose the local government to the uncertainties of the money market.
- *Diversion of earmarked funds.* Using earmarked funds for other purposes means, of course, that a future obligation to replace the diverted funds has been created, adding to future revenue needs.
- *Use of one-time revenues.* When a revenue available only in a single year (say, from sale of municipal property) is used to finance a continuing cost (such as salaries), the inevitable result is to create a budget gap the following year.
- *Roll-over.* Some local governments have responded to a shortage of funds by "rolling-over" into the next fiscal year bills and payrolls payable at the end of the fiscal year. This either increases funding requirements for the next year or leads to the continuing practice of rolling over end-of-the-year bills.

These practices are facilitated by accounting methods that obscure their impact upon the financial condition of the local government. As a result, deficits are hidden. This is not possible if the government follows generally accepted accounting practices (GAAP) in reporting its financial condition. This is because GAAP requires that financial results reflect not only income and outgo but also the net change over the year in specified assets and liabilities. Deferring payment of end-of-the-year bills, for example, has no effect on the deficit or surplus because the increase in outstanding bills as well as actual disbursements are included in the calculation.

These accounting practices, discussed more fully in chapter 6, set the rules for balancing the budget. They cannot, of course, identify in advance the proposed budget balanced through manipulation of revenue and expenditure estimates; in such situations, there is no substitute for careful scrutiny and analysis.

The Budget Process

Public officials engaged in budgeting often refer to the "budget cycle" as a short-hand way of describing the sequence of events that is an important characteristic of the process. A simplified graphic description of the principal events in the budget cycle is shown in exhibit 3–3. The following sections briefly describe what happens during the major phases of the budget cycle.

Preplanning and Policy Guidance.   The preparation of a new budget begins well in advance of the beginning of the fiscal year—by as much as twelve months in many localities. The principal actors in this first phase of budget preparation are the central budget staff and the chief executive. The budget staff begins its work by formulating rough estimates of revenue availability and expenditure requirements. If, as is usually the case in most communities, it looks as though demands for services and the cost of meeting these demands will exceed anticipated revenues, the budget staff will begin identifying places to cut back. In those fortunate localities which expect to have extra revenues available, planning can also focus on what would be appropriate expansions or additions to municipal services—or how best to reduce the tax burden on the citizenry.

Discussion of these prospects with the chief executive leads to the formulation of a preliminary budget strategy. Targets for expenditure reduction and revenue increase are identified and weighed as to priority. Additional information needed to make sound budget decisions is identified. These strategic thoughts are often presented in the form of a guidance letter or memorandum from the chief executive to agency heads. The letter usually notes how difficult the budget prospects appear to be, identifies key policy issues on which more analysis is desired, and may ask for optional presentations of expenditure requests to give the chief executive more policy choices.

Preparation of Estimates.   With the dispatch of the guidance letter, two parallel processes of estimate preparation begin.

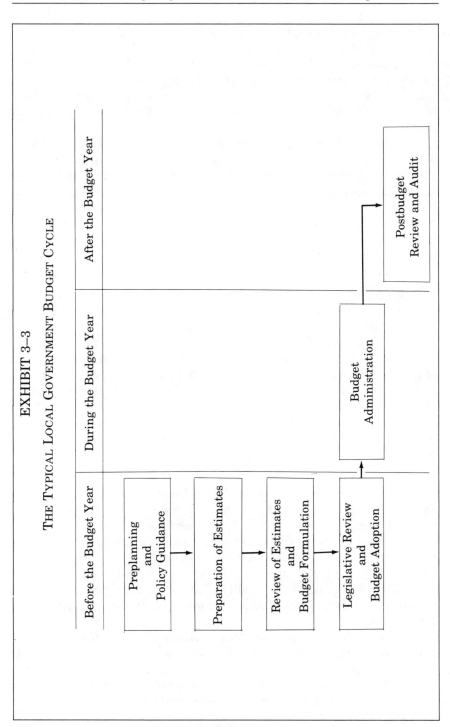

EXHIBIT 3-3

THE TYPICAL LOCAL GOVERNMENT BUDGET CYCLE

Before the Budget Year

Preplanning
and
Policy Guidance

Preparation of Estimates

Review of Estimates
and
Budget Formulation

Legislative Review
and
Budget Adoption

During the Budget Year

Budget
Administration

After the Budget Year

Postbudget
Review and Audit

The process that concerns revenues is usually confined to the central budget staff and a few other agencies that play a role in revenue generation. The tax collection agency, units that collect fees for services such as water and sewer service and, possibly, separate units that focus on intergovernmental aid are among the lonely group that tries to forecast what revenues will be available to support the local budget in the next fiscal period.

Each operating agency has the responsibility for preparing estimates of its own expenditure needs. In many cases, the receipt of the chief executive's guidance letter kicks off a parallel process within each agency as the agency head directs his own staff units to start analyzing their needs and priorities for internal agency review. Typically, three to six months are consumed in agency activities dealing with preparation of estimates. The process culminates with submission of the estimates to the chief executive and the central budget staff.

Review of Estimates and Budget Formulation. Once agency budget estimates are on hand, the central budget staff begins a review process to identify more precisely how difficult it will be to balance the budget. This process usually includes intensive scrutiny of agency requests, back and forth discussion with agency personnel to clarify issues, and identification of the critical choices that will confront the chief executive.

The culmination of this phase of the budget cycle is the preparation of the executive budget. This represents a melding together of anticipated revenues and estimated expenditures into a balanced package based on decisions by the chief executive. Executive review and budget formulation normally takes from one to three months.

The Fiscal Year. While many localities adopt a fiscal year that is the same as the calendar year, many find it more convenient to adopt fiscal years that begin on April 1, July 1, or other dates. Sometimes, there are several fiscal years within a single jurisdiction—for example, in cases where the local government and the school board prefer different starting dates. Additional complexities arise where the state government's fiscal year differs from that of the locality. The federal fiscal year, which now begins on October 1, adds another complication to local budgeting and accounting.

Because of the importance of intergovernmental aid in most local budgets, it is essential that local budget planning take these different time frames into account. When uncertainty arises as to the future level of state or federal aid—which may not yet be appropriated as the local fiscal year begins—it is often essential to prepare contingency plans to deal with possible shortfalls.

Legislative Review.   Once completed, the executive budget is submitted to the local legislative body for its review. In most localities this review process involves public hearings as well as internal reviews by legislative committees and staffs.

The concept that citizens as well as public officials should participate in the budget process has gained considerable strength in recent years. Nearly all local governments provide for some form of citizen participation in the budget process. In most cases, the point where the opportunity for participation occurs is when the legislature holds a public hearing after receipt of the executive budget draft and prior to adoption.

In some larger localities, the process of citizen participation begins early in the budget cycle and continues to its end. This is the case, for example, in Dayton, Ohio, and New York City; both have established formal processes for citizen involvement throughout the budget cycle.

Budget Adoption.   The legislature makes its own decisions on what changes it wants to make in the executive proposal and then adopts the budget. This is normally done a month or more before the new fiscal year begins.

Budget Administration.   Once the fiscal year begins, the major outlines of expenditures and revenues are controlled by the adopted budget. However, the real world is difficult to control and unforeseen events such as national economic changes or local emergencies can force revisions in local budgets. In addition, no budget can foresee the nature and timing of the detailed changes that take place as municipal employees resign or retire and prices for goods and services rise. The precise schedule for filling vacant positions or defining exactly what supplies will be purchased is left in most communities for budget administration rather than being set precisely in the adopted budget. Individually, these changes may not affect the budget significantly, but collectively, they may add up to major pressures that must be carefully watched and controlled to maintain budget balance.

Postbudget Review and Audit.   With the end of a fiscal year another aspect of the budget cycle begins. This consists of developing more precise data on just what happened during the year and how the final budget condition compares to the original adopted budget. The comparison involves detailed analysis by accountants and auditors. It provides information that is useful both to meet sound standards of fiscal performance and also as an input to the preparation of subsequent budget forecasts.

Summing Up: The Budget Process

This chapter has described the essential features of local budgeting. They include the executive budget concept and the roles of different officials in the process as well as the key functions that budgeting serves: control, management, and planning.

The local budget is really made up of several budgets: operating, capital, and at times, others (such as CDBG) as well. Budget balance is the requirement that sets the framework of discipline that, in turn, gives rise to many of the important financial information needs.

Budgeting is also a time process. It begins before the fiscal year, involves important administrative actions during the year, and must be followed by a postaudit review.

These many dimensions of budgeting in turn create the need to link budgeting to the other local financial management processes discussed in later chapters.

A Modern Budget System 4

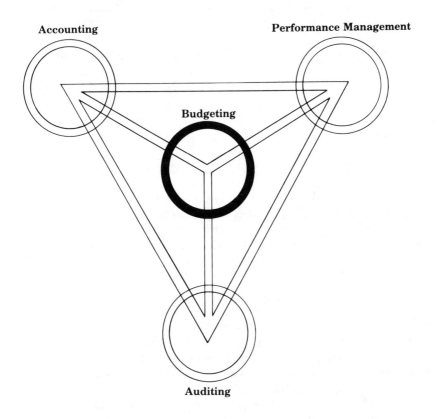

Accounting

Performance Management

Budgeting

Auditing

"means changes—"

This chapter is concerned with how the local government budget system ought to be structured. Budget systems that meet, to a very substantial degree, the standards we suggest here are already being followed in many American local governments. In fact, we have drawn heavily on the experience of those governments in writing this chapter.

A modern budget system depends upon much more than the skills and efforts of the central budget process. Indeed, this is the reason why so many attempts to upgrade the budget process have had disappointing results. Neither the analysis required for rational budget decision making nor the monitoring necessary to assure the implementation of the budget are possible without adequate information on expenditures, revenues, performance, and program results. Budget analysis is pointless unless it is used by the chief executive and legislators in making decisions. The new approaches analysis is likely to suggest are, in turn, scarcely feasible without the top level support and managerial accountability needed to carry them out.

The chapter is divided into two major sections, the first on budget decision making and the second on the administration of the budget.

The Budget Decision-Making Process

Budget decision making in most governments has been and, for the most part, still is incremental. By this, we mean that the budget is prepared by repricing last year's budget to reflect changes in wages and prices. Adjustments are made for added needs and obligations and for reductions due to reduced needs, economies, or, sometimes, more widespread budget cuts.

In some local governments, budgets are prepared using, at least in part, non-incremental approaches. The newer budget systems, such as the Planning-Programming-Budgeting system (PPBS) and Zero Based Budgeting (ZBB) are intended to systematize the scrutiny in the budget process of the expenditures in the base budget. The advocates of the new systems have tended to exaggerate the extent to which a nonincremental approach is feasible but there is little doubt that budget decision making in most governments could be substantially less incremental in nature and based, instead, on a more analytical, more searching review of proposed expenditures and revenues. The purpose of this chapter is to set out the elements of a modern analytically based budget process and how they can be implemented.

The promise of PPBS and other new budget systems introduced during the 1960s was rarely realized. The failure of these innovations in most jurisdictions was due to a number of factors including inadequate resources, the lack of a sustained multiyear development effort, limited managerial capacity in the operating agencies, and finally, the lack of an integrated financial management concept coupling budget reform with related improvements in accounting, performance management, and auditing.

While PPBS and ZBB failed in most jurisdictions as systems, they did achieve significant success in demonstrating the benefits of issue analysis and program analysis in budget decision making. The results are still evident in the vastly improved quality of budgeting in scores of state and local governments and federal agencies.

The development of a modern budget decision making system is not easy. It will usually take five years or more to make such a system fully effective. It will require changes not only in budget procedures but also in supporting information and management structures.

The discussion in the following sections covers the major elements of a system for rational decision making in the budget. These are

- A budget structure that facilitates analysis and decision making
- A capacity for analysis of budget issues
- A longer-term perspective
- Staffing for a modern budget system

Structuring the Budget for Decision Making

The structure of the budget determines to some degree how budget decisions are made. This can be seen most readily in a comparison between line item, organizational, and program budgets.

The line item budget directs attention to the bill of materials and the personal services to be financed under the budget. A budget structured by organizational units focuses on the amounts necessary to support the various departments and agencies of government.

The program budget, on the other hand, permits us to look at spending proposals in terms of the services they are intended to provide to citizens. In a program budget government operations are grouped by programs, each defined by the basic purpose it serves. One program might, for example, include all of the functions and operations intended to protect citizens against crime and enforce the law. Each program can be broken down further into subprograms, activities, or elements. For example, the program "law enforcement and protection against crime" might include "investigation of crime" as an activity or subprogram.

The advantages of the program budget can be best shown by illustrations from an actual operational budget system. Exhibit 4–1 shows the overall program structure used by Sunnyvale, California, which has one of the most fully developed local budget systems in America. The terms used for the various categories in the program structure differ from gov-

EXHIBIT 4–1

ELEMENTS AND SUBELEMENTS OF THE GENERAL PLAN:
CITY OF SUNNYVALE, CALIFORNIA

Elements	Subelements
1. Transportation	1.1 Circulation 1.2 Mass Transit
2. Community Development	2.0 Administration 2.1 Land-Use 2.2 Open Space and Conservation 2.3 Housing and Revitalization 2.4 Safety and Seismic Safety 2.5 Function and Appearance/ Public
3. Environmental Management	3.0 Administration 3.1 Water Resources 3.2 Solid Waste Management 3.3 Sanitary Sewer System 3.4 Surface Runoff
4. Public Safety	4.0 Administration 4.1 Law Enforcement 4.2 Fire 4.3 Support
5. Socioeconomic	5.1 Health and Well-Being 5.2 Social Services 5.3 Economic and Employment Services 5.4 Education
6. Cultural	6.0 Administration 6.1 Recreation 6.2 Library 6.3 Historical Preservation
7. Planning and Management	7.1 Fiscal Management 7.2 Community Participation 7.3 Legislative 7.4 General Management 7.5 General Support 7.6 General Services Support 7.7 Redevelopment

ernment to government and Sunnyvale uses a somewhat different hierarchy of terms than those used in the text above.

In Sunnyvale, the program structure is applied not only to the budget but also to the general plan—the broader statement of local policies and objectives—and to all of the financial and performance aspects of both the plan and the budget. Sunnyvale's program structure is, in fact, the organizaing principle for all major government decisions. Exhibit 4–2 provides a more detailed breakdown of two of the Sunnyvale elements. Each component of the program structure is defined by supporting statements specifying its purpose, objective, or mission and each is related to condition and performance measures. The purpose, objective, or mission becomes more concrete and specific as one moves down the hierarchy from the broadest category (*Element* in the Sunnyvale structure) to the narrowest (task) category.

A program structure is merely a set of categories or pigeonholes into which the budget is divided. However, when these categories are defined in terms of their purposes, it is possible to relate the amounts budgeted to targets or expectations of the extent to which the purposes are to be achieved and, where appropriate, to estimated workload and output.

Sunnyvale divides subelements into programs each of which has a single program-wide objective. The objective for the street maintenance program in a recent budget, for example, was as follows:

> Maintain 590 lane-miles of street surface in a safe, attractive condition for $1802 per lane mile.

Program service objectives are defined at the subprogram level. There may be several such objectives for each subprogram. One for the fire services program is illustrative.

> Provide on-scene services to requests within four minutes 95% of the time.

At the lowest level, the task, the focus is on the number of production units or output to be performed with a specified input of manpower and other resources.

The Sunnyvale program budget relates costs to the quantity and quality of performance and its effectiveness in meeting its ultimate objectives. The Sunnyvale approach is unusually elaborate and is feasible only because of efforts previously made by that community to measure and report on performance. (This is discussed in chapter 7.) A local government just beginning to develop program budgeting could not, of course, replicate Sunnyvale's performance in its initial years, but there is no reason why this could not be done gradually.

The key advantage of the program budget is that it organized budget

EXHIBIT 4–2

REPRESENTATIVE PROGRAMS: CITY OF SUNNYVALE, CALIFORNIA

3. Environmental Management Element

3.0 Administration Subelement

  301. Public Works Management
  302. Engineering Services
  303. Private Development Review

3.1 Water Resources

  311. Water Supply
  312. Water Distribution and Maintenance

3.2 Solid Waste Management

  321. Solid Waste Disposal System

3.3 Sanitary Sewer System

  331. Sanitary Sewer Maintenance
  332. Water Pollution Control

3.4 Surface Run-Off

  341. Storm Drain Maintenance

6. Cultural Element

6.1 Recreation Subelement

  611. Aquatics and Swim Center Maintenance
  612. Community Center Management
  613. Neighborhood Recreation Activities
  614. Physical Recreation Services
  615. Special Recreation Services
  616. Tennis Activities
  617. Special Groups Recreation

data in a form conducive to the analysis necessary for rational decision making. If we view the budget as a set of decisions on the purchase of goods and services to be provided to the citizens of the community using their collective resources, then the program budget focuses attention on those goods and services and the purposes or needs they seek to serve.

The program budget provides the basis for linking the services to be delivered by government with the cost of providing them. The first questions of any buyer are "What will it cost me?," "What am I getting for the money?," and "What will it do to me?" These are the "bottom line" issues which program budgeting seeks to address. Budget analysis, discussed in the following section, goes even deeper into these questions.

Analysis in the Budget Process

In preparing its annual budget, a local government must answer a series of questions like the following:

- How much money are we likely to have to spend during the budget period?
- How much will we need for obligations we have already incurred?
- What would it cost to continue existing programs at present staffing levels?
- To what extent is it possible to reduce those costs by making our operations more efficient or through savings?
- Are there programs that, even when efficiently managed, do not yield benefits equal to their costs?
- What increases do we face in costs under legally mandated programs?
- What are the highest priorities of the community in terms of discretionary services including possible new programs as well as increases in existing programs?
- How much do we need to save to cover possible future contingencies?
- What can and should we do about taxes? Do we have leeway to cut taxes or add new programs?

The answers to many of these questions are not obvious even to experienced budget examiners. How, for example, does one determine what can be done to make local refuse collection more efficient? Or, whether crime can be reduced by expanding the police department? Or, what is likely to happen to local revenues if the economy declines?

Many of these issues cannot be satisfactorily resolved without extensive fact-finding and analysis. Even though the ultimate decision is usually judgmental, budget analysis defines the options and risks on which judgment is based. Without analysis, the usual course is to follow established practice; this may be an unconscious decision to continue programs of questionable efficiency and effectiveness.

Of course, there are limits to our ability to apply analysis. Not all problems have answers. Furthermore, it is not feasible to undertake an extensive analysis of each of the hundreds of expenditure and revenue issues in the annual budget. Some selectivity is necessary simply because of the limits on analytic resources and the time and attention of decision makers. Moreover, for most major local programs, detailed analysis should not be necessary more often than, say, once every four or five years. Many lesser programs are not important enough to warrant committing the resources required for extensive study.

The burden of analysis is too great to be done exclusively by the staff of the budget agency within the few months during which the budget must be prepared. Much of the work can and should be done prior to the date on which agency budget submissions are due. A plan for the analytic work should be made soon after the last budget has been transmitted to the local legislature. The plan should define the major issues to be considered in the next budget and assign responsibility for the work required. For some complex matters, even longer lead times may be required.

Responsibility for analysis should not be limited to the budget staff. Operating agencies should be required to take responsibility for analysis of major management and program issues within their jurisdictions. This might be done jointly with budget staff or, at times, with the help of consultants. This is more than a matter of supplementing the limited manpower available from the budget staff. It should be an integral part of an effort to make the heads of operating agencies accountable for the efficiency, effectiveness and quality of their operations—as discussed in some detail in chapter 7.

Even an expanded analytic effort of the kind described will not meet all of the needs of the budget process. The range of potential issues and the number of activities and programs are simply too great to expect more than selective coverage of high priority issues. To help in meeting the need for analysis there are other potential sources of information and analyses relevant to budget decisions. The most important of these is the audit program. Audits that are designed to include management audits and program evaluations can make a substantial contribution to budget decisions. This is especially so if the audit program is focused on programs and functions of special interest and concern. This use of the audit is discussed further in chapter 9.

Information on cost and performance is as important as analysis. Indeed, without an adequate information base, analysis becomes, at best, difficult and expensive and, at worst, impossible. On the other hand, a well-designed information system will both facilitate analysis and make some types of analysis unnecessary. Financial management information systems that can help support analytic efforts are covered in chapter 8.

Budget decision making cannot rise very much above the average level of management in the local government. It will reflect the quality of local information systems, the adequacy of the audit program, and the performance demanded of agency heads as well as the competence of the budget staff. Analysis is significantly strengthened when it is linked to other financial systems, such as the audit and improved information processing.

Types of Analysis. Exhibit 4–3 identifies seven different types of analysis that can enter into the process of budget preparation. The different kinds of analysis are not wholly separate from one another; however, an analysis of a given program may, for example, involve elements of forecasting, pricing, management analysis, program evaluation, and market analysis.

The determinations involved in three of the seven analytic processes (forecasting, pricing, and strategic planning) must be made in every budget process. Management analysis, program evaluation, market analysis, and investment analysis, on the other hand, are options in the sense that it is perfectly possible to complete the preparation of a budget without looking into questions of efficiency, effectiveness, or community attitudes or investment policy. Many local governments tend, in fact, to prepare budgets with little or no analysis of efficiency and effectiveness and rely largely on intuitive judgment to assess community attitudes.

Costing or Pricing the Budget. In many budget agencies, the principal task of budget preparation is to reprice the existing level of programs and operations to reflect changes in prices and wages. Repricing is a largely mechanical process and can even be performed by computer once the new price and wage levels or the percentage increases in existing levels are specified.

Common price assumptions used throughout the budget should be developed as part of the forecasting process. Wage and salary levels for the budget preparation by either collective bargaining or unilateral legislative action, but often, estimates must be included in the budget prior to completion of collective bargaining. This poses difficulties since the amount tends to be treated by union officials as the opening bid from which bargaining begins.

With a continuation of high rates of inflation, the repricing of the budget often raises issues for management analysis to identify opportunities to reduce the use of inputs, especially personnel and energy, for which price increases tend to be particularly large these days.

EXHIBIT 4–3

ANALYSIS IN BUDGET DECISION MAKING

1. **Pricing**	Determining resource needs for existing and proposed programs given forecast factor costs.
2. **Forecasting**	Budget year estimates of • Revenue under current and alternative revenue structures • Factor costs including prices of purchased supplies, services and equipment, interest rates and salaries, and wages • Program demands, needs, and workload • Contingency reserves and factors to cover possible errors in forecasts
3. **Management Analysis**	Identifying opportunities for cost reduction through improved management, changes in work organization, investment in plant and equipment, contracting-out services, and other measures.
4. **Program Evaluation**	Evaluating costs of programs and activities against their effectiveness in achieving ultimate objectives and identifying more cost-effective alternatives where appropriate.
5. **Market Analysis**	Determining the desires and preferences of the community with respect to existing programs, perceived needs for improvement, and proposed new programs.
6. **Investment Analysis**	Analyzing current and future costs and benefits of capital investment in terms of discounted present values.
7. **Budget Strategy**	Making the final budget choices based on an explicit statement of the pros and cons of alternative approaches.

Forecasting. A budget is a future plan based on forecasts or developments during the budget period that may be entirely or in large measure beyond the control of the government preparing the budget. Forecasting may be a problem of limited importance in smaller local governments, but in larger-governments, sound forecasting can be critical to the viability of the budget.

Most important and most difficult is the forecasting of those revenues that are sensitive to changes in economic conditions. Personal income and payroll taxes, business income and gross receipts taxes, and retail sales taxes are the most important of these.

A small but increasing number of local governments subscribe to commercial economic forecasting services to help in revenue forecasting. A few have their own econometric forecasting models. Most still predict revenues on a judgmental basis heavily dependent upon past and current experience; the results are often as accurate as those achieved by more sophisticated methods. Regardless of the methodology, major errors in forecasting tend to be concentrated at turning points in the business cycle.

There are other areas where forecasts must be routinely made. Estimates of probable wage and price levels are one example. Another case includes the many estimates of the need, use, or demand for a wide range of services ranging from school enrollment to requests for police, fire, and ambulance services. Often, one can safely assume that year-to-year changes will be small and that programs can readily adapt to differences between actual and estimated levels. This is not, however, always so. In addition, there is the special problem of forecasting demand for new programs.

Forecasting public assistance and medicaid expenditures has proved difficult for those local governments responsible for these programs. This is important because all eligible applicants must be served and because the amounts of money involved tend to be very large. Local trends are typically more important than changes in the national economy.

The capital budget depends upon forecasts of needs for longer periods in the future. Projected changes in population and its age composition are very important in these forecasts. Many communities continued building new schools and additional recreational areas up to the very peak in school age population—despite declining birth rates.

At a minimum, a forecast is a statement of what is expected to happen in the future; for example, "sales tax revenues for fiscal year 1982 will be $12.1 million" or "wage costs will be $9,600,000." For variables of high importance to the budget, a forecast should have the following characteristics:

- An explicit statement of the factors that contribute to the forecasted result
- The separation of factors that can be controlled or influenced from factors that cannot be controlled
- Presentation of the results as a range, with one point in the range identified as the most likely result
- A clear and understandable explanation of the linkage between current or recent actual experience and the forecast

A forecast constructed this way gives the decision makers who use the forecast an opportunity to evaluate the uncertainty and risk involved in acting on the forecast. In addition, because no forecast can be wholly relied on, reserves to cover possible revenue shortfalls or new expenditure requirements are highly desirable as are contingency plans for expenditure cuts or even tax increases during the year.

Management Analysis.   Management analysis focuses on the relationship between resources used and the output of goods and services produced. The purpose is to increase program efficiency or to improve program effectiveness. In the context of budget preparation, the identification of oppportunities to reduce costs tends, of course, to be the most important objective. Most local governments have significant opportunities to improve efficiency or effectiveness. Yet, management analysis has often been neglected in local budget preparation.

We have suggested earlier that the analysis of a significant number of management issues is unlikely without a plan for such analyses formulated well in advance of budget preparation and enlisting the staff of both the budget staff and the operating agencies. A major responsibility of the budget staff is the identification of issues and opportunities. The management of a local government program may become an issue by virtue of citizen or council complaints or observed performance problems. The identification of other opportunities for improving performance depends upon either a professional study of current performance or an analysis measuring local operations against best practices or performance elsewhere.

While the analysis of the issues may be done by others, the budget should develop the recommendations for action in the budget. These recommendations must deal realistically with the time required to effect managerial changes, the additional resources needed for expert assistance, new equipment and the like, and the administrative measures required to assure implementation.

Budget review provides an impetus for management improvements but much more is clearly required. The best approach is a management plan, incorporating performance targets and schedules, regular reporting and monitoring, and linked to the budget process. Chapter 7 discusses this subject.

Program Evaluation. Program evaluation is intended to determine the effectiveness of programs in achieving their objectives. Evaluation typically requires an independent after-the-fact examination of programs that cannot be conducted either by budget staff or as part of the budget process. Evaluation is sometimes done as part of a comprehensive or management audit (see chapter 9).

Evaluation is most important with respect to those programs aimed at changing the behavior or situation of persons affected by the program. Special education programs, manpower training, social services, and crime prevention programs are all of this character. Evaluations attempt, for example, to determine the effect of manpower training on the jobs and incomes of trainees, or of additional police on the level of serious crime. The issues of program effectiveness, which are discussed in chapter 7, are among the most difficult in local government. Evaluation data for some programs are crucial in budget decision making because they address the fundamental issue of the value of a service in relation to its cost.

Market Analysis. Market analysis would appear at first to have little relevance to local government. In fact, market analysis is potentially extremely important to the budgeting and management of government services and programs.

Governments and private businesses both provide services to the public. A business which fails to meet the price, quality, and convenience standards of its competition is unlikely to survive long. Governments, on the other hand, usually do not sell services but, rather, finance them from taxes and other revenues. For many services, the government is, moreover, the only provider within its geographic jurisdiction. As a result, there is usually no market test of the need or demand for government services or of the satisfaction of those who use those services. Market analysis is a means of better adapting government programs to the needs and desires of citizens.

Several key questions are involved:

- *How does the demand for services compare with supply?* Underutilized hospital beds, waiting lines for community tennis courts, declining book withdrawals in the libraries, and a backlog of requests for duplicate birth certificates are illustrative cases of imbalances between supply and demand suggesting either unsatisfied demands or wasted resources.
- *Are services provided under conditions and at times that satisfy user needs?* For example, even though total library use is declining, more

detailed data may show increasing utilization during Saturday and evening hours, suggesting a possible need to adapt hours to citizen demand.

- *Are citizens satisfied with the quality of the service provided?* Citizen complaints often indicate areas of dissatisfaction where additional resources or better management is needed. Citizen opinion surveys may provide a broader measure of satisfaction.
- *Is there a substantial demand for services not currently being provided?* Community opinion surveys are the best source of such data.

Elected officials have always done an intuitive kind of market analysis and attempted to respond in budget making to areas of citizen demands and complaints. A more systematic and analytical approach to the same problem offers very significant potential for improving the responsiveness of the budget and the government to citizen needs.

Investment Analysis. Investment analysis is applicable chiefly to capital budget decisions. The purpose is the assessment of an expenditure involving future costs and benefits. The techniques of investment analysis are well developed. Expected future costs and benefits are most often compared in terms of present value which is calculated by discounting future costs and benefits by the same rate of interest.

Local governments have tended to make limited use of investment analysis chiefly because most local capital investments seem either unavoidable (such as school construction) or to involve uncertain future benefits (such as economic development projects).

But there are, in fact, a wide range of local capital decisions where investment analysis can be helpful. Among them are the following:

- Construction or purchase vs. lease or lease-purchase for both real property and equipment
- Life cycle costs under alternative equipment replacement policies
- Investment in cost-saving equipment, facilities, or system development
- Weighing costs vs. benefits of added features on planned facilities
- Evaluating urban development projects in terms of the character of development likely to generate revenues sufficient for cost recovery
- Comparing costs of preventive maintenance vs. benefits of longer equipment life
- On discretionary projects, analyzing discounted costs and benefits of the investment

High continuing inflation rates have made investment analysis more difficult but they have, at the same time, greatly increased the need for such analyses.

Budget Strategy. Budget choices are disciplined by the scarcity of resources, the knowledge that the government cannot afford to do everything at once. One must decide between increasing taxes and cutting expenditures, or between cutting taxes and increasing expenditures. Decisions must be made on how expenditure cuts (or increases) are distributed among programs. The decisions are necessarily judgmental, the equivalent of an individual's choice between apples and oranges.

Budget choices are best made if they are based upon an explicit statement of the pros and cons of alternative approaches. Decision makers are greatly helped if they know the benefits and the number served by each of the programs involved. Some knowledge of citizen attitudes and desires can be very useful. However judgmental, the final budget decisions should not be uninformed.

In making budget choices, the one-year framework of budgeting creates a significant bias in favor of new expenditures and against reductions. This comes from the fact that the start-up costs of new or increased programs tend to be half or less of full annual costs while, similarly, the full savings from management improvements can rarely be realized in the initial year. New capital expenditures can be incurred with no costs to the taxpayer until later years when debt service must be paid. Maintenance of capital plant can be deferred in favor of more politically attractive expenditures. As this suggests, there is a need to make the choices on the annual budget within a longer-term perspective—a subject discussed in the next section of this chapter.

Multiyear Financial Planning

Most budgets contain specific recommendations for raising spending money in the next fiscal year. A multiyear plan is, by contrast, a tentative statement of future directions subject to substantial change before decisions must finally be made.

The multiyear plan should be developed as a means of examining the implications for the future of decisions already made, of current trends and likely future developments, and of alternative proposals for future action. The planning horizon may extend ten or twenty years into the future, but planning will be most useful for the period extending no more than three to five years beyond the next fiscal year.

The most important aspect of this intermediate range planning is the identification of post budget year effects of actions already taken and of commitments already outstanding. These include

- Debt service on bonds already outstanding or authorized
- Operating costs for staffing and operating new facilities

- Added cost of full-year operation of new programs initiated in the budget
- Amortization of accrued unfunded pension liability
- Replacement of one-time financing with permanent revenues
- Savings from the phase-out of programs and operations and productivity improvements
- Contractual cost increases due to collective bargaining, leases, and other contracts

A second category of future requirements would include necessary actions yet to be initiated. For example, many communities are faced with the need to close land fills, install air pollution control gear on incinerators, introduce advanced sewage treatment facilities, or take other mandated actions. There may be additional needs, sometimes ordered by the courts, the state government or the federal government, to upgrade other types of facilities.

Many local governments have multiyear capital expenditure plans. These should reflect a standard replacement cycle for fire apparatus, trucks, and other durable equipment and a similar schedule for repaving streets and modernizing or replacing obsolete facilities. There may be needs, especially in growing communities, for sewer and water extensions. Economic development, a major concern in many localities, typically requires some capital investment.

Multiyear planning for changes and improvements in operating programs is less common but can be very valuable. Productivity and performance improvement programs function best under longer-term plans because they often require capital investment and nearly always take significant time for implementation. New services for which there is a strong demand can often be implemented only gradually. Building adequate fiscal reserves is, similarly, almost always a multiyear effort. The effort should recognize that an elaborate planning process will not be productive in some program areas where future needs can be assumed to be much the same as current requirements.

Pricing future plans has become difficult given the uncertain future rate of inflation. It is, perhaps, best to initially formulate plans in terms of current dollars stated as increments or decrements to current budget levels. The totals can then be inflated by appropriate price increase factors.

It is important that revenue and expenditure prospects be tested under alternative assumptions with respect to inflation and economic activity. In many local governments, inflation tends to increase expenditures much faster than revenues. Without continuing growth and development, tax increases or service reductions may be inevitable. Where this is likely, a good multiyear planning process will identify the need for curtailing new commitments and trimming costs before more drastic changes are required in a crisis atmosphere.

Staffing the Budget Process

The discussion may appear to suggest that modern budget analysis depends upon the recruitment of experts from a wide range of different disciplines and professions. In fact, most of the staff needs can be met by generalists, perhaps supplemented by the occasional use of expert consultants.

Recent graduates of university schools of public management, public policy, and public administration have been trained in many aspects of the analyses mentioned here and have been exposed to a wide variety of public sector problems. The graduates vary, of course, in overall competence and in analytic bent, but, as a group, they constitute a major source of talent for local budgeting. Schools of business and management provide training in much the same skills, usually, however, without education in public sector operations and problems.

In the shift from a traditional budget process to more analytical approaches, additional staff is usually necessary. On the other hand, reductions in staffing existing budget functions may be possible, especially where the line budget is currently used.

The process will work best where the major operating agencies are also provided analytical staff. With such staff in the agencies, the effects on agency practices are likely to be faster and communication better.

Budget Administration

The review, analysis, and enactment of the budget would be a futile exercise if the government agencies fail to live within their appropriations. This is why the first stage of budget reform in American local government fifty to seventy-five years ago focused primarily on the development of effective machinery for controlling expenditures.

Expenditure control is, however, only one aspect of budget administration. Effective implementation of the budget demands not only adherence to expenditure limits but also the achievement of the program performance objectives reflected in the budget. In most American governments, these performance objectives have tended to be neglected in budget administration.

The realization of the performance objectives in the budget is discussed not here but in chapter 7. It is important, however, that these objectives be kept in mind in considering the fiscal aspects of budget administration. Procedures for expenditure control and budget modification have often been impediments to the achievement of program performance objectives.

This need not be so. Performance management and expenditure control can and should be designed to realize both aspects of the budget program. The task of budget administration, even if limited to its expenditure aspects, is as much a matter of management as of control. Budgetary decision making does not stop with the enactment of the budget but continues through budget administration as the budget is adapted and modified to reflect unanticipated developments. The preparation of the budget is a planning process; budget administration is, on the other hand, a matter of helmsmanship dependent upon early identification of problems and obstacles and timely action to surmount them.

The performance of the accounting system is crucial. Effective budget administration is possible only with accurate, current, and adequately organized information on expenditures, encumbrances, and revenues. The actual implementation of controls on spending is, in large part, the responsibility of the accounting department. The role of accounting is the subject of chapter 6.

The budget cannot be a rigid prescription for the use of local resources over the twelve months of the budget year, except, perhaps, in very small and stable communities. It is, rather, a plan based on assumptions about community needs and resources during the budget period. Some of these underlying assumptions will, inevitably, prove to be incorrect in some respects. The deviations between budget assumptions and projections, on the one hand, and actual developments, on the other hand, are ordinarily of minor and manageable dimensions; sometimes, however, the course of events will be such as to have major unanticipated impacts on the budget.

This should not be surprising. Economic forecasts by the most highly regarded experts have often been far from the mark, especially at turning points in the economic cycles. Local revenue estimates based upon assumed changes in price, incomes, and business conditions are necessarily fallible. So are estimated expenditures for programs, such as public assistance, that are sensitive to changes in the economy. Mother Nature contributes additional uncertainty. Every year, hundreds of local governments incur unexpected costs due to heavy snowfalls, floods, hurricanes, or tornadoes. Riots, demonstrations, public disorders, and major fires may be very expensive in terms of emergency service costs. Anticipated federal or state aid may vanish with new legislation or as the result of the rejection of a local grant application. Court orders or new federal or state requirements may impose unexpected financial burdens.

Future uncertainty has become increasingly important in local budgeting, especially in the larger cities and counties. In part, this is due to increasing reliance on income, payroll, sales, and other income elastic revenues at a time when the national economy has become increasingly volatile. In part, it is also due to the impact of continuing high inflation, to the pressures of collective bargaining with unionized public employees, and to the special hazards of intergovernmental financing.

To cope with these problems, the budget must be monitored to assure early identification of revenue shortfalls, expenditure increases and emerging problems. New incremental requirements not anticipated in the budget must be analyzed and recommendations made for their disposition. Expenditure and revenue estimates must be adjusted to reflect changing circumstances throughout the year.

The primary objective of budget administration is to keep expenditures in balance with resources while accommodating unanticipated high priority requirements. In most localities, budget administration also serves a number of other objectives, including

- Maintenance and support of governmentwide systems (such as telephone, data processing, printing and reproduction, central purchasing) and policies to deal with known but not readily predictable expenses (such as the use of overtime).
- Provision of safeguards against wasteful or questionable expenditures of funds, either generally or in areas of special vulnerability or concern.
- Assurance that the budget is implemented in a way that is consistent with the intent of the legislative body and with executive representations to the legislature.

These secondary objectives tend to call for greater involvement by the budget agency in the review of individual transactions than might be necessary solely to keep expenditures within available resources.

The Tools of Budget Administration

Procedures for the administration and control of the budget vary widely among local governments. This is due largely to differences in the basic form and structure of local budgets. There are several different procedures or tools for controlling the budget. The following are the most important:

Apportionment or Allocation of Funds. In many localities, funds from budget appropriations and other authorizations are not available for spending until they have been apportioned or allocated by the budget agency. There are several reasons for this

- For continuing programs and operations, some means is needed to assure that appropriations are not overspent and are so managed as to support operations through the entire fiscal year. A local government cannot easily close down its school system or police or fire department in midyear. As a result of this problem, many local governments allocate or apportion appropriations by quarter or month over the course of the fiscal year.

- Year-end spending rates must be held to levels consistent with the budget for the subsequent fiscal year. This problem of "annualization" can be seen clearly in the following example. An increase of $150,000 in the current appropriation for salaries and expenses would finance ten additional employees at an average of $15,000 per year for a twelve-month period. It would pay for twenty additional employees at the same salary for six months (if they were hired halfway through the fiscal year). In the latter case, a total appropriation of $300,000 would be required in the next fiscal year to carry the new staff, even without any change in salaries. To avoid "annualization" problems, controls on expenditures or obligations are often supplemented by limits on the total number of jobs that the agency can fill.

- The spending plan must provide for contingencies. There may be shortfalls in revenues or increased expenditure requirements to cover emergencies or unanticipated increases in open-ended programs. Some local governments have adequate reserves or budget allowance for contingencies. Others—including those with the greatest fiscal problems—do not have adequate reserves or allowances. They often find it necessary to hold spending below appropriation levels so as to accumulate savings as a cushion against possible adverse developments.

- It may be desirable to withhold funds appropriated for new projects or programs until the administering agency has detailed its plans for the new activities.

- Program appropriations where responsibilities are divided among two or more agencies must be allocated among the agencies involved before they can be spent.

Modifications of the Budget. Changes in the budget are necessary throughout the year in most local budgets. The number of such modifications is greater under the line-item budget where even within-grade promotions may require budget modifications. Most modifications can be effected administratively by transfers of funds from one account to another or from one line to another within a single appropriation account. The basic rule under which these modifications can be approved is that increases in expenditures in a given appropriation account or line item must be offset by decreases in another account or line item. This assures that total authorized spending does not exceed the amount in the budget as initially enacted by the legislative body.

Legislative approval is usually required for changes that increase the aggregate amount of the budget and for interagency transfers of funds. In some jurisdictions, legislative approval is required for all or a substantial proportion of all budget modifications, including changes of a routine character and little budgetary significance.

Personnel Controls.   In most local government agencies and programs, wages, salaries, and fringe benefits constitute the greater part of expenditures. In these cases, limitations on the number and salary classification of agency jobs can be an effective means of expenditure control. Usually, agencies can employ personnel only in positions included in an approved table of organization or specified in the budget schedules, if a line budget is used. The budget may, however, not provide sufficient funds to fill all positions. The task of accommodating to budget limitations may be left to the discretion of the operating agency. Often, however, the budget agency imposes specific limits on the number of positions that may be filled or even requires budget approval of every new hire. Hiring freezes, now common in local governments in straitened fiscal circumstances, represent a special application of this approach.

Other Controls.   In some localities, budget agency approval is required for all contracts for goods or services or for all over a specific maximum amount. In others, only certain specified contracts are subject to budget approval. Computers, data processing services, automobiles, space rental, office equipment and furnishings, and telephone services are among the goods and services to which special controls are often applied.

Cost-Effectiveness of Budget Controls

The controls placed upon the expenditure of budget funds may involve costs of very substantial magnitude, including

- Expenditures for staff engaged in budget control in both the budget agency and the operating agencies
- Costs incurred as a result of delays in the processing of requests for budget agency approval
- The effect on program costs and effectiveness of restrictions on managerial flexibility that prevent or discourage optimal approaches in agency program management
- The development of an environment hostile to initiatives that could result in productive innovation

These costs are widely recognized. Indeed, they underlie frequent complaints about the budget process by program administrators at all levels of government.

The key question for chief executives and legislators is whether it is possible to reduce these costs without significant sacrifice of budget control. In most jurisdictions, the answer should be affirmative:

- The objective of overall budget control can ordinarily be achieved through quarterly apportionment of expenditures supplemented, where necessary, by limits on the aggregate number of filled positions.
- Budget review of contracts, the filling of individual positions and other specific transactions is the most burdensome and least productive type of control. It can usually be eliminated or limited to special cases with little, if any, adverse impact on fiscal control objectives.
- Control at the line-item level generates a large volume of budget modifications, most of which have little or no significance for the budget or local policy.
- Governmentwide policies can often be enforced, without the review of individual transactions, merely by requiring demonstration of compliance to be included in the voucher file as a condition of payment.
- Where the likelihood of noncompliance is low and its significance limited, timely ex post auditing is frequently the most cost-effective control method. The cost of preventing all noncompliance may be far greater than its value.
- Budget review of individual transactions and line-item modifications frequently represents not the application of standard policies but the use of *ad hoc* budget agency judgments as a substitute for clearly articulated policies.

A simplified and effective budget control system can serve to focus the energies of the budget agency staff on matters of more central importance to the budget mission. It can also have positive effects in encouraging responsible management in operating agencies.

This is not a universally held opinion, however. In some jurisdictions, budget agencies hold on to detailed control and advance approval of even minor changes.

Safeguards Against Deficits

The budget should allow reserves, contingency allowances, and other means to protect against at least the normal hazards of budgeting. A local government should, for example, make provision to cover possible revenue shortfalls attributable to the difficulty of forecasting the economic downturns that have tended to occur twice or more a decade. On the other hand, most local governments cannot be expected to accumulate reserves sufficient to weather—without tax increases, expenditure cut-backs or borrowing—the fiscal disaster that may occur in the one year in perhaps a century that everything goes wrong.

The amount needed to provide a prudent cushion against adverse developments has become much larger under the economic conditions that have prevailed since the early 1970s than it had been during the earlier part of the postwar period. Needs will vary among localities depending upon the characteristics of fiscal structure and of the community. The following are among the most important factors:

- The extent to which the locality is dependent on taxes for which collections vary sharply with economic conditions such as those on business income, personal income, payroll, gross receipts, and sales
- The vulnerability to changes and the likelihood of significant changes in federal and state grant policies
- The importance of open-ended entitlement programs (public assistance and medicaid) in the local budget. Many counties but few cities have such responsibilities
- The past incidence of emergency-related, unanticipated expenditures (such as snow removal or police overtime)
- The potential for reducing expenditures, if necessary, in the last half or quarter of the budget year

It is worthwhile, especially in communities with high fiscal vulnerability, to test the budget under "worst case" assumptions drawn from experience during the last decade for each major budget element subject to significant variability. This is likely in some local governments to indicate a substantial risk exposure and the need for reserves equal to 5 percent or more of the budget. That need can be reduced in the course of the budget year.

Some local government charters or applicable state laws provide for accumulation of specific reserves to cover possible budget deficits. The unexpended balances of appropriations are, in the typical case, transferred to the designated reserve until it reaches a specified amount, often stated as percentage of general fund reserves or of the real property tax base.

A second arrangement designed to prevent deficits is the inclusion in the enacted budget of a specific allowance for later supplemental appropriations.

Budget staff in some local governments build in protection against possible expenditure overruns and/or revenue shortfalls by routinely overestimating expenditures and underestimating revenues. The resulting allowance for contingencies, because it is not identified, is hidden from those likely to urge its expenditure for new or expanded programs or higher employee salaries. A reserve may be accumulated from such annual surpluses, but, more commonly, the estimated surplus will be appropriated to help finance the budget of the subsequent year.

In local governments under increasing fiscal stress, these conservative practices tend to be gradually abandoned. Reserves are committed to financing the budget while the cushion in the revenue and expenditure estimates is progressively reduced. These governments become increasingly endangered by adverse changes in the economy and other external factors.

The Responsibility Center

The organization of an effective system of budget administration begins in the operating agencies where most financial commitments are initiated. The key is the designation of the agency officials with the authority to make and the responsibility for financial decisions.

This is not a complicated matter. Generally, the official with responsibility for the management of a major program should also be entrusted with the responsibility of administering the finances of that program. This official is then properly accountable for both *program performance* and *fiscal performance*.

This approach requires the division of an operating agency into *responsibility centers*. These responsibility centers should be the major organizational units of the agency. They will tend to vary in the character of program responsibilities. Some may cover the administration of a single major program while others involve multi-program assignments. The agency budget and finance unit might be designated as the responsibility center covering all central staff and service units. A small agency might constitute a single responsibility center and smaller organizational units in larger agencies can be combined in a single centrally administered responsibility center.

Responsibility for *budget administration* should follow agency organization. Budget analysis, preparation, and presentation, on the other hand, are most effectively done on the basis of programs and activities. If the budget is based strictly upon programs defined in terms of basic purpose or objective, it will be necessary to allocate appropriations among responsibility centers where more than one major organizational unit is involved in carrying out the program. There is a tendency to exaggerate the differences between program and organizational structure. The correspondence between the two is, in fact, usually fairly close with relatively few exceptions.

Administering the Capital Budget

The administration of the capital budget poses a substantially different set of problems than those raised by the operating budget. Separate appropriations are usually made for larger capital projects, but many cities follow a practice of appropriating "lump sums" to finance groups (or programs) of smaller capital projects such as those involved in park or building rehabilitation or water line replacement.

There is a wide variation in the role in administration and control played by the budget agencies and other governmental units with respect to capital budgets. In many localities, planning agencies are responsible for much of the process of preparing the capital budget and multiyear program; public works agencies may be responsible for reviewing plans for capital projects designed by private architects and engineers working for the locality under contract. In other localities, there is an engineering unit within the budget agency which reviews plans and cost estimates at various points in the development of a capital project.

The control process for captial projects—which begins once a capital project has achieved approved budget status—is concerned primarily with two interrelated features: cost and timing. The two are closely related because, in these inflationary days, the more time that passes in the design stage of a capital project, the more costly it becomes. Communities across the nation have become painfully aware of this problem as, again and again, the original cost estimates for capital projects escalate markedly before they can be completed.

There are three principal points in the "life cycle" of a capital project where control can be exercised.

Scope Approval.   The first major control point occurs before architectural or engineering design when the scope of a capital project is specified. The scope of a capital project is specified. The scope is a description of the project in terms of size (number of square or cubic feet), special features (equipment, materials, facilities), and other characteristics. A scope can be a very simple, one-line description that refers to standards (such as a 7,500 square foot, one-story branch library) or it can be a highly detailed, book-length description of what the architect or engineer is asked to design. The scope is also used as the basis for the initial detailed cost estimate.

Design Approval.   When the design has been substantially completed, it can be reviewed for consistency with the scope and its cost can be reestimated on a more accurate basis. One reason for the review at this point is to be sure that "extras" have not crept into the design—as the public client for the building is tempted to upgrade its contents. Another reason is that this is likely to be the last point at which reductions in the scope (to cut area or volume or substitute less costly materials or equipment) can realistically be made to compensate for escalating costs. The later such cuts are made, the more likely they are to delay design, subjecting the project to even more inflationary pressure.

Construction Award.   Only when the design is complete and competitive bids have been received (if the project is to be built by outside contractors) is there firm knowledge about cost. Control at this stage is difficult to apply because cost-reducing changes will extend the design time further—but if the project's cost has gone beyond the available funds, there may be no other choice.

Depending on the project there may be additional (or fewer) appropriate control points. Projects to be constructed by "in-house" staff will probably not be as readily subject to advance cost controls, because there is no firm construction contract. Rehabilitation and reconstruction efforts often encounter unforeseen difficulties, such as unexpected on-site problems. Construction projects may also encounter difficulties that are hard to foresee, such as delays in relocating site tenants, material shortages, and strikes.

One approach to improved control in dealing with the time factor (that, in turn, helps control costs) is through project management techniques and time-focused information systems (see chapter 7).

A final factor to be taken into account in the administration of the capital budget is financing. This can be most effectively planned when there is a meaningful capital construction schedule from which cash requirements can be determined and bond financing planned and scheduled. Uncertainty on the availability and cost of money can be relieved throught the sale of bonds prior to the initiation of the project, or at the earliest opportune time. The sale of bond anticipation notes for interim financing, on the other hand, extends the period of uncertainty by delaying the permanent financing of the project.

Summing Up: The Modern Budget Process

Budget decision making can be and often is guided by "what was done last year." Better budget decision making requires much more:

- A budget structure that places decisions in a program context
- The analysis of issues necessary to identify the most cost-effective approaches to achieving local objectives and the options available to decision makers
- The accounting and program data required to assess agency needs and performance

- Extensive information from audits and program evaluations
- A multiyear perspective of program effects and requirements

Decision making does not stop with the enactment of the budget and many of the same factors are important in effective budget administration. In addition, good budget administration depends upon

- Accurate and prompt reporting of the financial and program data needed to monitor the budget
- The capacity to modify and adapt the budget to changing conditions
- An effective budget control system that does involve substantial costs through delays and impediments to managerial flexibility

In budget administration, the interrelation with accounting and performance management is critically important to effective operation.

Linkages Between Budgeting and Other Fiscal Systems 5

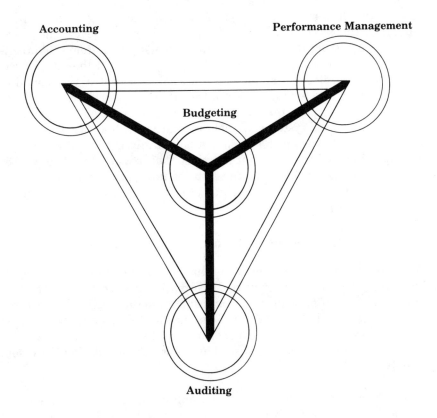

Accounting

Performance Management

Budgeting

Auditing

"the way to integration"

The two preceding chapters have described the many ways in which the budgeting process is involved in public decision making. In this chapter we want to center the discussion on the concept of "linkages" among the different components that are essential to a full-fledged financial management system.

The "logo" at the top of this page illustrates these linkages in graphic form. It shows at least one way to view the four basic component financial management systems and the six major linkages among them.

In the diagram, we've shown budgeting in the central position among the four systems in the drawing because we find it useful to think about financial management as revolving around the decision making that takes place in the budget process. But that's only one way to see it. The accountant or comptroller for a locality might well draw the illustration differently. He (or she) might prefer to see accounting in the center. Similarly, the management staff responsible for the development and operation of the locality's performance management system could legitimately view its operation as central and supportive of the other three. And in the eyes of the local auditors, they have the central responsibility to check up on and evaluate each of the other three systems.

This isn't a dispute that needs to be settled. However one wants to view the four basic systems, we believe that you'll find that each of the six possible linkages among them is a potentially important aspect of a locality's financial management functions. This chapter briefly describes each of these six linkages because we believe that a fully integrated system involves them all. Subsequent chapters will further expand on these relationships.

Budgeting and Accounting Linkages

There are two important functions that accounting performs for budgeting: First, it provides most of the information needed to keep track of how closely local financial operations conform to the budget plan. Second, it plays an equally important role in the control of local spending by checking on the validity of expenditures as they are made. These are sufficiently different functions so that it's worth considering them separately.

The Information Function.   Once the annual budget has been adopted by the local legislative body and the new fiscal year begins, financial transactions must be recorded and reported in such a way that the budget staff can keep track of how well they're doing against the financial plan. Without such information, the budget staff would be unable to take timely action to offset the adverse effects of shortfalls or to prevent overexpenditure of appropriations. It is the responsibility of the accounting sytem to provide this "how we are doing" information on a periodic basis.

The accounting system must also provide the data on current and past program expenditures and costs that the budget agency needs in the preparation of the next budget. If the accounting system is to play its management reporting function, it must be capable of collecting and displaying data in a form that is readily usable by budget staffs. Unfortunately, this is easy in principle and, at times, very hard in practice. This is because accounting tends to focus on what was done with municipal money (most easily tracked by objects of expenditure and organizational units or responsibility centers) while budgeting focuses on the purpose for which it is to be used (best measured by functional programs and activities). In theory, these are wholly compatible, but in practice they're sometimes difficult to coordinate.

Introducing the program and activity structure needed by budget analysts into the accounting system makes its operations more complex and costly. In theory these demands can be overcome by a correctly coded, computerized accounting system—but our surveys indicate that this is a target as yet not reached by most local governments.

In a sizable proportion of local governments, accounting information has limited value for budget administration, either because it is not provided promptly, because the categories in which it is available are not useful, or because expenditures are understated by virtue of the large "float" of transactions between agencies and the accounting unit. Exclusion from the total of some types of encumbrances or obligations may add further to the understatement.

These problems in the accounting-budgeting relationship are discussed further in chapter 6, together with some indications as to how they can be resolved. Chapter 8 tells how some advanced localities have linked their accounting and budgeting systems through integrated computerized systems.

The Control Function.   The control of expenditures to assure that appropriations and apportionments are not exceeded is normally carried out, not by the budget agency, but by the accounting staff. It is the responsibility of the accounting system to make sure that purchase orders and contracts are not approved and payrolls are not disbursed unless there is an appropriation with sufficient unencumbered balance against which they can be recorded. The accounting staff must also assure that expenditures are charged to the correct appropriation and that they have been properly approved and documented.

Budgeting and Performance Management Linkages

The budget "plan" is a statement about what a locality expects to buy over the next year and how it expects to pay for it. The dollars on the expenditure side of the budget are related for each appropriation to certain planned expenditures (such as personnel or debt service). For example, a local budget might note that the highway department's street paving function will cost $500,000 next year (to buy the work-time of 20 members of paving crews and the asphalt they need to accomplish their mission).

This is a useful way to describe what the local government plans to do but it's only part of the picture. It's also important to know that the budget funds are intended to provide the resources needed to pave five miles of streets (or twenty lane-miles); if this target isn't achieved after the money has been spent on salaries and asphalt, the budget objective will have been missed even though spending on the function is kept within the allocated total of $500,000. Failure could occur either if less than five miles of street were paved or if the quality of the paving job was poorer than the accepted standard.

Failure to keep spending within the assigned constraints is an expenditure control (or accounting) problem while failure to achieve the assigned mission is a performance problem. It is useful to the city manager and the highways commissioner to know which problem they encountered because the knowledge may help them take corrective action. But failure is no less real because it can be allocated to the fiscal or the productivity aspects of municipal management. Both are important.

Good budgeting requires performance measures to help assess whether or not the missions of public agencies are accomplished. Linking performance measures to budgetary accounts is the most straightforward way to accomplish this end. How this can be done is discussed in chapter 7.

Budgeting and Auditing Linkages

Budgets look forward in time while audits look back to see what's happened. The linkages between them grow out of these different "clocks."

There are two different kinds of audit that provide different—but equally important—forms of feedback to the budget process. These are the financial and performance or management audits.*

Financial Audits. The financial or compliance audit is intended to determine whether the financial transactions of the local government have been properly reported and classified, whether internal controls are sufficient to justify confidence in the reported data and whether legal requirements have been complied with in the expenditure of funds. As auditors pore over the records of local programs and operations they are likely to raise tough questions about how closely actual spending—by amount and purpose—adhered to the budget plan. In responding to these

---

*While we prefer the terms "financial" and "performance" to describe these two basic types of audit, chapter 9 also defines them in terms that are used by the General Accounting Office, the principal federal audit agency.

questions, the central budget staff and operating agencies are likely to gain useful insights into where their procedures can be improved and their control processes tightened.

A subsidiary, but nevertheless important, aspect of this type of audit is to provide the chief executive, the local legislature, and the general public with assurance as to the soundness of their financial systems.

Performance or Management Audits. This type of audit—which as yet has been adopted by few local governments—examines whether public programs meet their performance objectives. The performance-oriented audit provides a detailed look at what has actually happened as a result of budgetary expenditures. Did the program operate as planned or did it fall short because of some unanticipated difficulty? The auditor's independent position outside the line of responsibility for operating the program lends credibility to his findings. In addition, a good audit report will include recommendations for changes in the way a program is operated worthy of consideration both by agency managers and by the central budget staff.

The ways in which audits link to the other fiscal processes are discussed in chapter 8.

Accounting and Auditing Linkages

The financial audit is an essential underpinning to a sound accounting system as well as to good budgeting. First, it determines (usually on the basis of review of a sample of all transactions) whether obligations and expenditures were accurately recorded. Second, it assesses the adequacy of procedures such as those used to authorize and record financial commitments (often referred to as the "internal controls" of the accounting system).

An audit is, for all practical purposes, impossible unless the accounting system is auditable. The accounting system must be designed to leave an audit trail that permits the tracing of transactions through the documentation that supports them. It should have explicit procedures that establish the pattern of accountability and provide the auditor with an understanding of how the system is intended to operate. An audit of an accounting system without these characteristics cannot do a complete review of sample transactions; it can only report the basic deficiencies in the accountability system.

Accounting and Performance Management Linkages

Some of the measures of local government performance can be derived directly from a properly designed accounting system. This applies primarily to measures that are directly determined in dollars, the basic unit of the accounting system. For example, a useful indicator of performance in revenue collection by a water and sewer agency might be the dollar receipts resulting from payments by customers. This could be derived directly from the accounting system in most communities.

In most cases, however, the accounting system provides only a portion of the data needed by a performance management system. The dollar measures of the accounting system must be supplemented, in practice, by direct measures of input (such as man-hours or truck-shifts) and of output (such as tons or square yards of asphalt laid) that are rarely included in the accounting system itself. While there is nothing in theory that would prevent an accounting system from recording nondollar data, the practice in government has been that accounting systems record primarily items measured in dollars but few of the other items needed for a broad-based performance management system.

There are other problems besides the fact that the key information pieces are missing that make difficult the task of relating accounting system information to the concerns of a performance management system. Unless the accounting system is carefully designed with the input and output concepts clearly in mind, it is likely to prove of little use in measuring productivity. In fact, this was the situation that we found during the surveys of local government performance management systems conducted during the preparation of this volume; few relied on the local accounting system for much data. The problem arises because, in most situations, the primary data categories utilized in the accounting system—normally objects of expenditure and large organizational units—are not a suitable basis to generate data that can be related to the performance management system. In addition, most local budget and accounting systems record, at best, only part of the costs associated with public activities.

The aspect of accounting that has the most direct relevance to a performance management system is usually called "cost accounting." A cost accounting system is specifically designed to record and report data on the full costs of programs, projects, and activities. Past accounting is essential to the computation of the cost per unit of selected city services.

This is a demanding requirement. It means careful advance planning by accountants and performance analysts to define the principal units that will be used in the performance management system.

Performance Management and Auditing Linkages

There are ways in which a performance management system can be useful in the audit process and vice versa. These mutually reinforcing relationships are now briefly described. But before describing them, we have to acknowledge that, to date, the benefits that these two systems can derive from each other are still largely hypothetical. During our review of actual practice, we found very few instances of localities which had *both* performance management and performance audit systems in being.

The performance management system, just as other governmental activity, ought to be subject to periodic audit. The purpose of the audit is to assess where the system meets acceptable standards of accountability and control. This has been done in some localities but usually by a fiscal research or civic body (rather than a certified auditor) because a principal purpose of the audit was to build credibility in the productivity system's accomplishments.

A second relationship between audits and performance management can arise where a municipality has a performance management system in being. In such a case, the mission statements and performance indicators establish a highly useful body of data for management and performance type auditing, giving the auditor a solid base of standards against which to gauge agency accomplishments.

Summing Up: Six Linkages on the Road to Financial Integration

This chapter describes the ways in which the four basic financial management systems can—and should—be linked to one another. Some of these linkages are more critical than others, but a locality that wants to obtain high fiscal marks needs to consider all six linkages.

The next three chapters in this volume focus directly on the three fiscal systems which are essential to support a strong budgeting framework: accounting, performance management, and auditing.

Accounting and Control 6

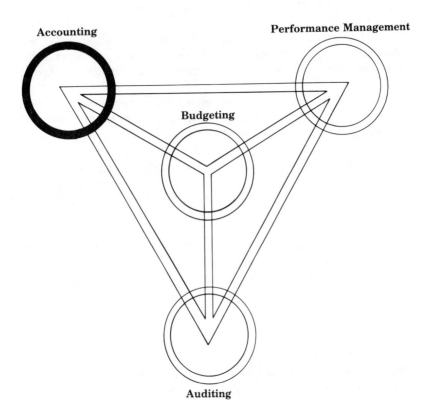

Accounting

Performance Management

Budgeting

Auditing

"In revenues, expenditures, number of employees, and assets, a local government will often be larger than any private business within its boundaries."

In the great majority of local governments, responsibility for accounting and disbursement is centralized in a department of finance or accounting. Sometimes, this department also includes the budget and/or audit functions. A centralized finance department is the point in local government through which all transactions flow and are recorded, at which all payments are made, and through which most funds are received.

Accounting serves three basic purposes, all fundamental to building a basis of confidence in the handling of public money:

1. *Control.* Accounting is the basic element of the financial control structure. It is the means by which commitments and expenditures of public funds are limited to the amounts and purposes authorized in the locality's budget.
2. *Accountability.* The accounting system also incorporates the procedures by which financial commitments are made and reviewed, the assignment of responsibility and accountability, and the internal controls necessary to the integrity of the system.
3. *Information.* Accounting is the single most important system in local government. In most instances, it is the *only* such system with comprehensive coverage of all agencies in the same terms and the same level of detail.

In addition, the accounting and finance department usually is charged with the related responsibilities for cash, investment and debt management, and for revenue collection. These are important functions, but they are secondary to the purposes of this guide and are not treated here.

The discussion below is organized under four topics:

1. Budgetary Control
2. Accountability and Internal Control
3. The Framework of Local Government Accounting
4. The Information Functions of Accounting

Budgetary Control

Limitations on spending are, of course, initially set by the amounts provided in the budget as enacted by the legislative body and, sometimes, by other continuing authorizations for expenditures for certain specified purposes. Expenditure limitations may change over the course of the year as the result of the issuance of budgetary apportionments and allocations, the approval of budget modifications, and the enactment of supplemental appropriations.

The implementation of these limitations depends first on compliance by the various agencies of the local government and, ultimately, on enforcement by the accounting or finance department. Conceptually, the implementation of accounting controls to enforce budgetary limits on expenditures or obligations is a relatively simple matter. The amount available for expenditure in any account is specified by the appropriation or other legislative authorization as modified by budgetary allocation or apportionment. When the balance available is inadequate to cover a proposed expenditure, the accounting department usually returns the voucher to the agency with a statement indicating that sufficient funds are not available.

The performance of the control function should satisfy three basic standards:

- The effective application of budgetary controls
- The prompt and accurate recording of transactions
- Expeditious processing to avoid undue delays in contracts and payments

These standards are routinely met in many local governments. In many others, they are not. The major problem tends to be the time required for processing. The delays often have significant adverse effects on program performance and on costs. Poor performance, where it occurs, is usually due to overloading the accounting control function. This involves problems of two different kinds.

In the first case, the local government may be attempting to exercise control at a level that is too detailed to permit effective and efficient operation. This not only adds to the number of units subject to control but also tends to result in an improportionately large increase in the number of budget modifications. Supplementary controls on spending for certain objects and budgetary apportionments may add to the problem. The situation is worst in governments with line-item budgets since line-item control maximizes the number of both controls and budget modifications.

The second problem arises from the accounting review of transactions for purposes other than the enforcement of appropriation limits. This is discussed in the following section.

Accountability and Internal Control

A local government will often be larger in terms of revenues, expenditures, number of employees, and assets than any private business located within its boundaries. Assuring the proper custody and management of local resources is a major responsibility.

The discharge of this responsibility depends, in part, upon what accountants call a system of internal controls. Internal control is defined by the American Institute of Certified Public Accountants as follows:

> Internal control comprises the plan of organization and all of the
> coordinate methods and measures adopted . . . to safeguard . . . assets,
> check the accuracy and reliability of . . . accounting, promote opera-
> tional efficiency, and encourage adherence to prescribed managerial
> policies . . . . a "system" of internal controls extends beyond those
> matters which relate to the functions of the accounting and financial
> departments.*

It is not appropriate in this guide to discuss the problem of internal control in any detail except as it bears on the integration of accounting with other financial functions.

Effective internal control depends, first, on accountability—a clear-cut assignment of authority and responsibility to specific officials for spending decisions and the custody of resources. It will be noted that the accountability is also identified in this guide as a key aspect of both budget administration and performance management.

The second element of internal control consists of procedures and regulations governing the commitment and disbursement and receipt of funds and the acquisition, custody, and disposition of other assets. Such procedures establish standards for the documentation of transactions, for higher level approval, and for divisions for responsibility for certain functions to make sure, in effect, that the fox is not guarding the chicken coop; they include many other safeguards as well.

The third element includes the various means of assuring that the safeguards incorporated in the procedures and regulations are effectively implemented. This is a major concern of the independent audit. Internally, this purpose is served by internal audits, the review of individual transactions, reconciliation of bank and book balances, and many other measures.

The application and verification of safeguards is not a minor matter. Even in a small local government, the finance department, as bookkeeper and banker to the operating departments, will receive from the agencies thousands of documents annually including payrolls, contracts, leases, and other documents evidencing obligations, requests for payments to suppliers and contractors, and others.

For every transaction, there must be appropriate certification, documentation, or other evidence that

- The obligation or disbursement has been authorized by an agency official to which that authority has been given.
- The obligation or disbursement is documented to identify the character and quantity of the goods or services ordered.

---

*Codification of Statements on Auditing Standards 1–23 #320.09. American Institute of Certified Public Accountants, New York, 1979.

- Prior to disbursement, the goods or services have, in fact, been delivered.
- The obligation is for a purpose covered by the subject appropriation.
- Procedural requirements have been met (such as those for competitive bidding, central purchase of supplies, or civil service certification of new hires).

The role of the accounting agency varies. In many local governments, the accounting agency reviews every transaction not only to assure compliance with procedure and documentation requirements but also to evaluate the substance of the transaction. Preaudit, like the detailed line-item budget administration controls discussed earlier, may involve high costs without commensurate benefits. In the worst situations, preaudit introduces an unproductive second-guessing of agency decisions. In nearly all cases, it leads to significant processing delays.

A more efficient approach is to limit accounting review to assuring that the file includes the proper authorization and documentation. Even in this case, detailed review can often be limited entirely in favor of postaudits.

The Framework of Local Government Accounting

Before moving on to the information function of local government accounting, a detour of a somewhat technical nature is necessary to discuss standards for recording and reporting financial data. These standards involve the application of generally accepted accounting principles (or GAAP) which were developed by the accounting profession as a common set of rules for reporting financial information. The adaptation of GAAP to government has been done by the National Council on Governmental Accounting (NGGA) and published by the Municipal Finance Officers Association as *Government Accounting, Auditing and Financial Reporting* (Chicago, 1980).* It is usually referred to as GAAFR.

Generally accepted accounting principles are technical but they serve important and easily understood purposes. They provide, first, a common language that is necessary if financial reports are to be understood by bond underwriters and other outsiders. Second, they establish a standard for comprehensiveness of reporting that assures that all outstanding liabilities and obligations as well as assets are reported. Third, they provide a standard means for differentiating resources subject to special limitations. Last, they establish a prudent standard for the timing of revenue and expenditure recognition.

---

*This MFOA publication interprets NCGA's 1979 *Statement 1, Government Accounting and Financial Reporting Principles* and explains the revision from the 1968 version of GAAFR.

In addition, many states have issued accounting standards to be followed by their localities, and federal agencies issue standards to be applied to their grants. Not all of these are consistent with standards set in GAAFR. The current position of the National Council on Government Accounting is that where legal provisions conflict with GAAP, the local government should prepare its statements in accord with GAAP together with whatever supporting schedules are necessary to satisfy state law.

In the following sections, two of the most basic elements of municipal accounting are discussed:

1. *Fund structure* refers to the number and kind of different funds in which revenue is received and from which expenditures are made; and

2. *The basis of accounting* refers to the time and manner in which revenues and expenditures are recorded in the accounts of the municipality.

The fund structure and the basis of accounting are important with respect to both revenues and expenditures, whereas other aspects of the accounting system can be more meaningfully discussed separately for revenues and expenditures.

How Many Funds

Most private businesses account for all or most of their revenues and expenditures in a single general fund. Governments, on the other hand, nearly always use several different separate funds in addition to a general fund. This complicates government financial reports and budgets, sometimes making them difficult to read and understand.

Each fund is a separate accounting entity. A local government can, through its general fund, make properly authorized expenditures for any function the government is empowered to carry out except to the extent that functions have been assigned by law to some other fund. All other funds serve specified purposes and monies in those funds can be spent only for these purposes. In some cases, interfund transfers or loans can be authorized by the local legislative body.

There are good reasons for fund accounting:

- It assures the segregation of revenues and assets that are limited by law to certain specified purposes. For example, special assessments or earmarked taxes and revenues can't be spent except for the specific purposes allowed under law.
- It assures the separation of business-type operations that charge fees, such as a public water or electric utility, from the more usual government activity.

• It clearly separates resources that do not belong to the local government but over which it serves as trustee. Employee pension funds are a good example of where this separation is essential.

NCGA's *Statement 1* provides for three different categories of funds: (1) government funds, (2) proprietary funds, and (3) fiduciary funds. There are five kinds of government funds, two proprietary funds and four subclasses of trust and agency funds. The complete list is shown in exhibit 6–1.

Fund accounting makes sense for local governments but the proliferation of separate funds in some local governments is a matter for concern. A local government using a plethora of different funds can turn its financial statements and even its budget into a kind of jigsaw puzzle to be put together by the reader. The example in exhibit 6–2 describes the disappearance of the Department of Public Works in the Flint (Michigan) budget due to its division among several different funds.

Even the conservative 1968 GAAFR cautioned against the use of an excessive number of funds and the recent NCGA statement takes a similar stance:

> Governmental units should establish and maintain those funds required by law and sound financial administration. Only the minimum number of funds consistent with legal and operating requirements should be established, however, since unnecessary funds result in inflexibility, undue complexity, and inefficient financial administration.

Separate funds are necessary for trust and agency accounts such as pension funds, because the assets of these funds do not belong to the local government. Enterprise and intragovernmental activities are business-type activities for which separate funds are desirable. By and large, other types of funds are necessary only when required by law or when use of certain revenues is legally restricted to specified purposes.

The use of several different funds complicates the task of accounting since each fund must be subject to separate control. If the number of funds is not excessive, however, fund structure should have no significant impact upon the task of *expenditure control* since most separate funds would, in any event, be separate appropriation accounts. Fund structure does, however, have important effects on the broader task of *resource management*. This results from restrictions on the use of the resources and revenues of any specific fund for other purposes. For example, a shortfall in revenue received in the general fund cannot usually be offset by a surplus of earmarked revenue paid into the highway fund.

On the other hand, the use of multiple funds simplifies the job of control in some other respects. The usual types of expenditure control are often

EXHIBIT 6–1

TYPES OF FUNDS IN LOCAL GOVERNMENT ACCOUNTING

Government Funds:

1. *General Fund*—to account for all unrestricted resources except those required to be accounted for in another fund.
2. *Special Revenue Funds*—to account for revenues restricted to specified purposes—except special assessments, expendable trusts, and revenues reserved for major capital projects.
3. *Capital Projects Funds*—to account for resources segregated for the acquisition of major capital facilities—other than those financed by special assessments or enterprise funds.
4. *Debt Service Funds*—to account for the accumulation of resources for the payment of interest and principal on long-term debt.
5. *Special Assessment Funds*—to account for the financing of public improvements and services through special assessments.

Proprietary Funds:

6. *Enterprise Funds*—to account for operations financed and operated in a manner similar to private business enterprises, usually involving the provision of goods and services financed primarily from user charges.
7. *Internal Service Funds*—to account for the financing of goods or services provided by one government agency to another on a cost-reimbursement basis.

Fiduciary Funds:

8. *Trust and Agency Funds*—to account for assets held by a governmental unit as trustee or agent for individuals, private organizations, and/or other governmental units.

SOURCE: *NCGA Statement 1: Governmental Accounting and Financial Reporting Principles,* National Council on Governmental Accounting, 1979.

EXHIBIT 6-2

FINANCIAL INFORMATION IN FLINT, MICHIGAN

You Can't Find the Department of Works in the City's Financial Records

Flint's financial report for 1974—the year in which the city obtained a certificate of compliance from the Municipal Finance Officer's Association—contained 212 pages of data; to the city manager, the council, and the public, however, much of the data was not very useful. The report showed all the city's revenues and expenditures and the status of all major accounts of the city's thirty-six different funds. Yet it was difficult to read because, in accordance with standard accounting practice, financial information was not summarized by department or for the city as a whole. General funds, enterprise funds, trust funds, intragovernmental service funds, debt service funds, and other funds were each reported separately as if they had no relationship to each other.

The annual financial report was based on the financial structure of the city, which did not correspond to the city's organizational structure. If one wanted to know what was spent by the Department of Public Works, he would have to do a considerable amount of digging. (In fact, he would need more information than was contained in the annual financial report.) The result of this analysis would show that in terms of financial structure, the Department of Public Works showed up in six different city funds. Its $20-million annual expenditure would break down as follows:

Fund	Fy 1974 Expenditures (in $ millions)
General Fund	4.0
Gas and Weight Tax Fund	2.7
Public Improvement Fund	.7
Water and Sewer Fund	8.5
DPW Fund	1.6
Intragovernmental Service Funds	2.5
TOTAL	20.0

One would have found a little bit of the department in six different places. To complicate matters, each different fund was controlled by a different set of accounting and reporting rules. For example, the Water and Sewer Fund was an enterprise fund which presented information on a business-type income statement and balance sheet using full accrual accounting. The Gas and Weight Tax and General funds presented information on a revenue/expenditure basis, employing modified accrual accounting. The others were in between. If you looked only at the annual financial report or took information from the city's accounting system, you would not realize that the city of Flint was one governmental entity reporting to one city council or that its services were provided by departments, divisions, and agencies managed by managers within one organizational structure.

SOURCE: Brian W. Rapp and Frank M. Patitucci. *Managing Local Government for Improved Performance: A Practical Approach.* Boulder, Colorado. 1977. exhibit 39. p. 168.

inappropriate for, say, a municipal water department and it may be desirable to leave such a department free to conduct its operations from its own revenue much as it would were it a privately owned utility. Similarly, there is little point in expenditure controls that limit the authority of an employee retirement system to invest its resources. Fund structure helps in separating out activities for which routine, government-type budget controls are not satisfactory.

The Basis of Accounting

The basis of accounting is the most complicated aspect of this discussion of local government accounting. Yet, it is extremely important. GAAFR (1968) defined the basis of accounting as "a device for matching revenues and expenditures during a designated period of time and refers specifically to the time when revenues and expenditures are recorded as such in the accounting records."* The basis of accounting is reflected primarily in the way in which transactions are reflected in the government's financial statements. It has more limited applicability to the way in which funds are appropriated and controlled.

For governmental funds (see exhibit 6–1) through which most of regular operations of government are conducted, the modified accrual basis of accounting should be used. This means that

- *Expenditures* should be recognized in the accounting period in which the fund liability is incurred (if that liability is measurable) except for unmatured interest on general long-term debt and debt supported by interest-bearing special assessment levies.
- *Revenues* should be recognized in the accounting period in which they became available and measurable. "Available" means collectible within the current period or soon enough thereafter to be used to pay the liabilities of the current period.

Under this rule on revenue, property taxes (less an allowance for uncollectible taxes) would be recorded when levied. Most other local revenues are not measurable until the cash is actually received and would not be recorded until that time.

For *proprietary* funds, the accrual basis of accounting should be used following standard practice in commercial accounting. This involves not just a difference in the basis of accounting but in the focus of measurement. Expenses—the actual use of resources—rather than expenditures are measured. Expenses do not include expenditures for capital plant and equipment or inventories since these represent not resources used but additions to assets. Unlike expenditures, expenses do include depreciation

---

*GAAFR (1968), p. 11.

(to allow for the use of capital), the use of inventories accumulated during prior periods, and of goods and services paid for in prior periods. Undelivered orders are excluded since, of course, they cannot have been used even if paid for. Revenues are recognized when earned.

For *fiduciary* funds, either the accrual or modified accrual basis is to be used depending on the purposes of the fund.

The NCGA recommendations represent a sensible adaptation of accounting principles developed largely for private enterprise to the very different world of government. The modified accrual basis of accounting for governmental funds can be regarded as incorporating a desirable standard of prudence—recognizing spending commitments when they are made but deferring revenue recognition until amounts and availability can be determined. Meeting these standards should not be difficult for most local governments that now record expenditures at the time of commitment or obligation. For those localities using cash basis accounting, however, modified accrual accounting is a major and badly needed reform. If expenditures are not charged until cash is actually disbursed, neither effective control (which must be exercised when the spending commitment is made) nor an accurate reporting of financial condition is possible.

The use of accrual accounting for proprietary funds would mean, simply, that where the government is in the business of producing and selling goods or services, the results would be reported in business terms with a clear identification of any net income or loss.

The recommended practices are extremely important to financial reporting but have more limited impact upon budgetary control and appropriations. The NCGA specifically endorses encumbrance (or obligation) accounting for the control of governmental funds and suggests flexible budgeting for proprietary funds to permit adjustment to changes in demand.

The Information Functions of Accounting

The reporting of financial information is required to meet a variety of needs of users both within and outside the government. They include all of the following:

- Inernal uses:
  Budget planning and analysis
  Budget administration and expenditure control
  Revenue collection and receivables management
  Cash and investment management

- External uses:
  Comprehensive Annual Financial Report
  Grants reporting
  Other special reports

The character of the data needed varies among the different users and purposes. Meeting all of these needs requires a capacity to aggregate and report data at several different points in the transaction sequence (for example, encumbrance or obligation, receipt of goods and services, billing and disbursement) and under several alternative structures (rather than a single chart of accounts). The not insignificant technical problems of developing a financial information system with this capacity is discussed in chapter 8.

It is not necessary in this section to discuss all of the needs for financial information listed. Budget-related information requirements (including those for revenue collection) have been covered in chapter 4. Cash and investment management are important functions but, as we have already mentioned, are not treated in this publication. This section is, consequently, limited to two special needs for financial information and reporting that do not fit very neatly into other parts of the report.

The first of these is cost accounting which can be important to budget analysis, reimbursement and reporting under grant programs, and decisions on user charges. The second topic is the annual financial report which is critical to any external assessment of a local government.

Cost Accounting

Good planning requires good cost information. Cost accounting is a method for determining (1) the total costs, direct and indirect, of a program, project, activity, or operation, and (2) if appropriate, the cost per unit output of the goods or services provided. Meaningful cost analysis depends upon an accrual accounting system or—what amounts to the same thing—a capacity to adjust obligations or disbursements to an accrued expense basis.

Cost data are needed especially for programs where costs have a bearing on the amount of revenue generated. In grant-in-aid programs, particularly those of the federal government, reimbursements often cover the grantor's share of all costs if the grantee can identify them. Underclaiming of grant reimbursements is surprisingly common because of inadequate systems for measuring indirect costs. In the case of programs where the local government provides a service at a fee, cost information should be a basic input to the level of the fee charged. Even if the government elects to subsidize a service, it ought to know the amount of that subsidy. (See the example in exhibit 6–3.)

EXHIBIT 6–3

COST ACCOUNTING AND SUBSIDIZED SERVICES: FLINT, MICHIGAN

When Should the City Charge a Fee for Its Services?

The city of Flint provided a number of services on a fee-for-service basis. The most smoothly working example was the city's water division. The water division was established as a separate operating business (a public utility) within city government under the Department of Public Works. The fees charged for the amount of water residents used covered the total costs of operating the city's water and sanitary sewer systems, thereby ensuring a financially sound operation. Fees were established by the City Council, acting as a public-utility commission.

Other services provided by the city on a fee-for-service basis were not self-supporting. One example was the golf division of the Parks and Recreation Department. The golf division was recorded on the city's books as an enterprise fund; however, greens fees collected from golfers were set at a level that covered only the annual operating expenses of the golf courses. Neither the depreciation of the buildings nor the capital equipment used to maintain the golf courses was considered in calculating the fee. Therefore, the fees covered only part of the true costs, and the general public, through property and income taxes, unwittingly subsidized the remaining cost of each round of golf. The subsidy was hidden in the form of a budget appropriation to the park department as a whole; it was never clear how much the public was actually paying to subsidize each round of golf or each golfer.

Flint provided other services that met the criteria for placement on a fee-for-service basis. An excellent example can be found in the waste-collection and disposal division of the Department of Public Works. The service provided by this division was clearly identifiable; it could be measured in units; it was provided to individual property owners; and it was provided by a distinct and recognizable organizational unit. The city had ample statistical information to calculate the costs of this service for each customer on almost any use basis. Traditionally, however, waste collection and disposal was financed by a budget allocation from the city's General Fund. Administratively and organizationally, it would have been relatively easy to put this service on a fee-for-service basis, but politically it was not an acceptable idea.

SOURCE: Brian W. Rapp and Frank M. Patitucci. *Managing Local Government for Improved Performance: A Practical Approach,* Colorado, 1977, p. 164.

Where cost recovery is not involved, good cost data may still be critical. Local governments perform, for example, a host of activities that could be carried out under contract with private business, but determining the advantage of this, if any, requires accurate knowledge of costs. Unit cost data may also have value in reviewing programs of modest size and high appeal; programs, for example, such as service centers for teenagers, oldsters, and other special groups may sometimes appear in a far different light when converted to full costs per person served. Unit cost comparisons with other jurisdictions may be equally revealing. Finally, cost data provide much of the basis for setting performance standards.

Accurate cost accounting requires that both indirect costs and allocated costs be properly handled. Accounting for indirect costs (pensions, fringes, overhead) requires that they be consistently allocated among programs on a governmentwide basis. Accounting for allocated costs involves the distribution by program or project of the direct costs incurred by multiprogram organization units (responsibility centers). If a cost determination requires splitting the time of individual workers or small organizational units or purchases, the routine collection of such data may not be worth the effort. An alternative is to establish allocation factors from periodic sampling.

A depreciation allowance for the use of durable plant and equipment is another element of costs and requires the establishment of appropriate depreciation accounts and policies. Local governments have traditionally not depreciated plant and equipment (even GAAFR does not recommend the use of depreciation, save in enterprise and certain other funds), yet depreciation is a basic ingredient of cost analysis and not a major burden on the accounting system. (For a comparison of approaches to depreciable assets, see exhibit 6–4.)

The determination of cost per unit output requires not only cost data but also reliable measures of output. The problems of obtaining such measures are discussed in chapter 7. Obviously, since output measures will be valuable in cost accounting only if they are available for the same program and activity centers for which cost data are available, maintaining such consistency is an important purpose of integrated systems.

Annual Financial Reporting

The officials of a local government, like the officers of a publicly held corporation are stewards responsible for the management of resources that are owned by others—stockholders in the case of the corporation as opposed to taxpayers and citizens in local government. Governments, like corporations, also use resources that have been borrowed either directly or through the sale of bonds and notes to private investors. These important outsiders—citizens, taxpayers, bond- and noteholders and their

EXHIBIT 6-4

ACCOUNTING FOR DEPRECIABLE ASSETS: FLINT, MICHIGAN

There Are Many Ways To Finance and Record the Cost of an Asset

The city of Flint employed three different methods to account for the costs of equipment used to provide city services. Each method was tied to the way the city paid for the asset, and each resulted in a different cost calculation for providing the same service.

The first approach was to record the original cost of the equipment, not as an asset, but rather as an expense at the time of purchase. Such items were usually purchased under direct appropriation. Under the *direct appropriation approach,* city departments requested the purchase of equipment in their annual budgets in the full amount of that equipment's purchase price. If funds were available, the equipment was purchased; if they were not, a department made do with what it had. Once purchased, the equipment was used until it was no longer serviceable, at which time a request would be made for funds to replace it. Under this method, the annual budget of a department and the costs of the services it provided could fluctuate on the basis of whatever equipment was purchased in any given year. The disadvantage of this approach was that it often led to the use of outdated or obsolete equipment when the climate was not conducive to obtaining an appropriation for replacement. During the budget season, when cuts had to be made it was easier to postpone the purchase of a piece of equipment than to displace an employee.

The second approach also did not record the cost of the equipment as an asset which was then depreciated. However, this means of financing spread the cost over the years prior to the purchase. This *trust fund approach* was used primarily by the fire division. Under this method, the fire division would annually request a budget appropriation for the Fire Equipment Trust Fund in order to accumulate funds over a period of years sufficient to pay the large cost of replacing a fire truck or similar item when the time came to make such a purchase. With this approach, the annual appropriation was supposed to approximate the annual utilization costs of fire equipment. The approach may have been a reasonable one; however, it suffered from the disadvantage that an appropriation to a trust fund is an easy budget item to cut. Hence the trust fund seldom accumulated sufficient funds to meet equipment replacement needs as they occurred.

The third approach, used primarily by the police division and Public Works Department, was the *motor and equipment pool approach.* With this procedure, the motor and equipment pool purchased vehicles and equipment and then, in turn, rented them to city divisions and departments. The equipment purchased was recorded as an asset in the Motor and Equipment Pool Fund. Annually, the departments included the rental costs of the equipment in their budgets. During the course of the year, the divisions and departments paid the motor and equipment pool the costs of operating the equipment. The price paid by each department was the sum of operating costs, administrative costs, and depreciation.

Under this last system, the motor and equipment pool was able to accumulate funds that permitted the replacement of equipment when it deteriorated or became obsolete. At the actual time of replacement, a vote of the City Council was necessary to approve the purchase, but an appropriation was not required since money was already available in the fund. The annual budget of each department showed only the rental or annual cost of usage. This approach encouraged the timely replacement of vehicles and equipment, since the funds for purchasing the replacements could not be diverted to other purposes.

SOURCE: Brian W. Rapp and Frank M. Patitucci. *Managing Local Government for Improved Performance: A Practical Approach.* Boulder, Colorado, 1977, pp. 156–157.

agents—share a need for and a right to information on the operations and financial condition of the local government that is accurate, honest, and complete in its coverage of relevant data.

The primary means of conveying this information is the annual financial report. The National Council on Governmental Accounting has established standards and specifications for local government financial reports that are designed to assure that reporting is complete and unambiguous. These are set out in *Statement 1: Governmental Accounting and Financial Reporting Principles* (1979).

The NCGA sees the structure of financial reporting in terms of the pyramid shown in exhibit 6–5. The Comprehensive Annual Financial Report (CAFR) is the government's official annual report. The General Purpose Financial Statements (GPFS) are a part of CAFR that may be used in official statements for bond offerings and for wider distribution to users not requiring more detailed data.

The Comprehensive Annual Financial Report should be prepared and published promptly after the close of the fiscal year. It should include the report of the independent auditor (if an audit has been performed) and schedules essential to demonstrate compliance with finance-related legal and contractual provision. NCGA also recommends fifteen supplementary statistical tables to the extent they are appropriate as well as narrative explanations. Accounting policies and such other data as are necessary for a fair presentation in conformity with GAAP should be specified in notes to the financial statements. Budget appropriations and estimates must be reported along with actual results for the same period.

The rules of financial reporting may seem complex to the nonaccountant, yet the purpose and underlying concepts are both simple and sensible. The purpose is to provide an accurate and comprehensive statement of financial condition covering all of the significant assets and liabilities of the local government. Statements prepared according to generally accepted accounting principles are especially important in providing underwriters and prospective purchasers of the locality's obligations the information they need to make rational decisions. They are also valuable in any assessment of local finances, whether internal or external.

The underlying concepts are extremely important in understanding the financial condition of any given local government and in making comparisons among them. The key question is the extent to which resources used are funded by current revenues versus the extent, on the other hand, to which resources are provided by drawing down existing assets or accumulating liabilities for the future.

A few examples are illustrative:

- Two different local governments may have roughly similar reported rates of expenditure per capita. If, however, one is contributing to its employee retirement funds at an actuarily determined level while

EXHIBIT 6–5

THE FINANCIAL REPORTING PYRAMID

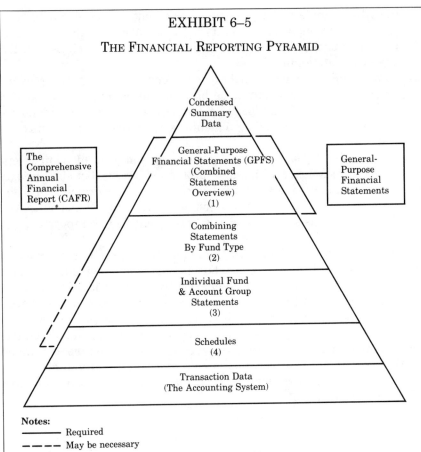

Notes:

———— Required

– – – – May be necessary

Levels of the Pyramid

(1) General Purpose Financial Statements (Combined Statements Overview)—provides a summary overview of the financial position of all funds and account groups and of the operating results of all funds. Also serves as an introduction to the more detailed statements and schedules that follow.

(2) Combining Statements (By Fund Type)—where a governmental unit has more than one fund of a given type (e.g., special revenue funds), combining statements for all funds of that type should be presented in columnar format. (In some instances, disclosure sufficient to meet CAFR reporting objectives can be achieved at this level; in other cases, these statements link the GPFS and the individual fund statements.)

(3) Individual Fund and Account Group Statements—present information on the individual funds and account groups where a governmental unit has only one fund of a specific type, or detail to assure disclosure sufficient to meet CAFR reporting objectives is not presented in the combining statements. These statements can also be used to present budgetary data and prior year comparative data.

(4) Schedules—are used: (a) to demonstrate finance-related legal and contractual compliance (e.g., where bond indentures require specific data to be presented); (b) to present other information deemed useful (e.g., combined and combining schedules that encompass more than one fund or account group, such as a combined schedule of cash receipts, disbursements, and balances [all funds]); and (c) to provide details of data summarized in the financial statements (e.g., schedules of revenues, expenditures, and transfers).

SOURCE: NCGA Statement 1: *Governmental Accounting and Financial Reporting Principles*. National Council on Governmental Accounting. 1979.

the other is underfunding its pension obligations, there may be substantial differences in real costs between them. Unfunded pension liabilities should be reflected in a balance sheet much as are, for example, outstanding bonds.

• Some local governments hold down expenditures by "rolling over" until the next fiscal year some bills submitted for payment at the end of the year. This, too, is a form of borrowing and should be reflected in the financial statements as an increase in accounts payable.

• On the other hand, some local governments may be added to assets not merely through accumulated surplus and reserves but also through reimbursements due from the federal or state government or even through excessive allowances for uncollectible taxes; under GAAP, these conditions should be consistently identified and reported.

Although we have emphasized the importance of the Comprehensive Annual Financial Report to external users, it should be evident that they should also be important to the chief executive and the legislative body. This is especially so with respect to year to year changes and trends over a longer period. A deteriorating financial situation, sometimes not fully evident to local government financial managers, can often be traced through changes in annual financial reports—if those reports are prepared under GAAP. A decline in reserves, increases in pension liability, higher reliance on short-term borrowing, and increases in accounts payable are among the indications.

Summing Up: Accounting and Control

The accounting and control functions of local government serve a variety of important purposes in an integrated financial management system. Serving all of these purposes effectively and efficiently is not easy. It requires

• The implementation of budgetary controls at a level that is not so detailed as to impede the expeditious processing of transactions
• Internal controls that are effective but do not depend upon preaudit or the detailed review of transactions prior to approval
• A capacity to produce the varied information required for budget analysis and administration
• Financial reporting meeting generally accepted accounting principles

Performance Management and Accountability 7

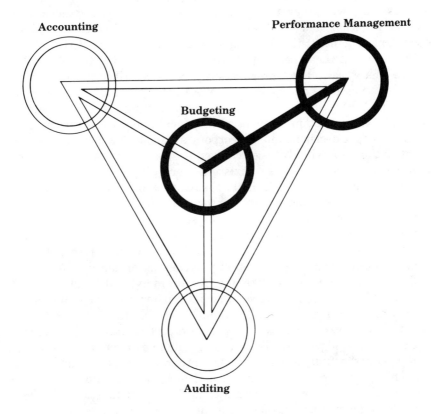

Accounting

Performance Management

Budgeting

Auditing

"beyond fiscal integrity"

Management and performance accountability is not usually discussed as a basic financial management function. Yet, a system for budget decision making and expenditure control would not be very meaningful unless it dealt with the need to make sure that the local government gets its money's worth in goods and services from its expenditures.

For most goods and services purchased from private vendors and suppliers, most governments require competitive bidding as a means of assuring the lowest possible price. Contracts awarded without competition are typically subject to procedures for review and approval designed to achieve the same objective. Governments—state and federal as well as local—have tended to be much more casual with respect to the efficiency and effectiveness of services they provide with their own employees to their citizens. Budget decisions on those services, more often than not, are based on "what they got last year" plus a little more for added workload or inflation or a little less because of either specific economies of operation or general fiscal stringency. Usually, there is little effort to make sure that the expected performance is achieved.

The analytical budget preparation process described in chapter 4 is intended to produce decisions that reflect both the need (or demand) for service and the most cost-effective means of meeting that need. However, without a continuing program of management and performance accountability, budget decisions must incorporate a somewhat speculative judgment on the results likely to be achieved—especially when those decisions involve significant changes in existing operations.

Performance management is the means by which a government introduces into its relationship with its program managers an understanding on future performance that serves the same purpose as a contract with a private supplier. It requires making managers accountable for achievement on a realistic schedule of specified targets with respect to the efficiency, quality, and effectiveness of program performance.

The government should, like any private individual or household, be able in its budget decisions to relate what it plans to spend to the services it expects to receive. It should, similarly, be able to relate what it has spent to what it has achieved in program performance and to compare both with its budget plan. To do this, it must be able to determine both budgeted and actual costs for the same programs, activities, and projects for which performance is targeted and measured. In other words, the budget, accounting, and performance management functions should be capable of generating data for the same group of program entries.

The chapter contains four parts. The first addresses the basic issues of how performance management can lead to increased accountability and better public service. The second focuses on the key role played by goals, objectives, and targets in a performance system for local government. Next, the chapter moves on to address the important questions involved in how to measure performance in the public sector. The last section has an organizational orientation; it describes some of the options available in setting up a performance system.

Management and Performance

In the search for better means of controlling and improving performance, many public officials have considered new approaches, such as program and performance budgeting, work measurement, and others. These management techniques seek three common objectives:

- Improved linkages between financial decisions and expected results
- Better and more systematic information on performance and results
- Greater accountability by program managers in achieving planned results

The process often starts when local officials begin to raise questions about the effectiveness and efficiency of government performance. Key questions are "How well are we doing?" "How much better could we do?" To answer these questions requires identifying the deficiencies, shortcomings, and problems in current performance and picking out specific opportunities for change.

Performance issues should not be separated from financial issues. The amount and quality of service that can reasonably be expected in any local program will, obviously, vary with the funding provided. Governments should always relate recommended budgets to planned levels and quality of service—but they often don't.

Achieving performance accountability requires that local government managers get clear signals as to what's expected of them so that they can be held responsible for the results they achieve. Accountability goes beyond fiscal integrity to address the issue of whether public funds are producing as much value as they might. Managers need to know if their activities are being carried out efficiently. Further, they need to improve their capacity to change and strengthen service delivery systems to make them more productive. This orientation on results characterizes the emerging modern management style, unlike the case in the past when the predominant focus was often primarily on inputs.

There are two basic aspects to a results-oriented approach:

- Using the budget process to decide on the quantitative and qualitative level of services the locality is able and willing to finance (How to do this is described in chapter 4.)
- Managing delivery of these services so that the desired levels of performance are in fact realized

This chapter primarily addresses the second issue. It describes how to develop and administer the setting of achievable performance standards and how to hold program managers accountable for realizing them. This isn't easy because

- Performance has many dimensions. It embraces efficiency, quality, and effectiveness. Each of these, in turn, may have several different facets
- Performance is often affected by factors outside the control of the responsible administrator
- These are real and important measurement problems that must be addressed—although their difficulty is sometimes exaggerated

Despite these problems, many local governments have created useful performance reporting systems and a number have moved beyond this point to establish effective performance accountability systems.

Performance reporting and accountability are basic ingredients of modern budget decision making and effective program management. Without performance data, program and issue analysis in the budget process is nearly impossible. Without performance accountability, there is no assurance that management will actually achieve the performance levels supported by the budget.

Goals, Objectives, and Targets

Logically, a local government starting out to develop a performance program should decide on the objectives it plans to achieve in each of its programs and operations. This is not simply a matter of deciding what local officials would like to achieve. To be realistic, objectives must be tailored to what is feasible. If additional resources are needed, the local legislature must decide if it is willing to provide the financing. Because it is rarely possible to do everything at once, priorities must be set among different objectives.

Priority setting and goal choosing can be approached in different ways. The classic place to start is with needs assessment and goal formulation—the "top down" approach. However, many jurisdictions start to develop performance measurement systems even before determining goals and needs. This may make sense—on a governmentwide basis or for particular agencies and programs—when it appears that better information on actual performance is necessary before realistic, achievable objectives can be set.

Here, however, we will follow the classic, top-down approach. This consists of four steps:

- Identifying problems and needs

- Formulating goals
- Setting objectives and performance targets
- Preparing action plans and timetables

Identifying Problems and Needs

The city of Sunnyvale, California, has a well-developed planning and management process that starts with an annual assessment of community conditions to help identify problems and needs. The assessment generates a set of community condition indicators for each major problem area. Some indicators (for example, population, lane-miles of city-owned streets and number of dwelling units) provide measures of the size of the "universe" with which the particular program is concerned. Other indicators (for example, the number of traffic accidents or dwelling units needing major repairs) measure the extent of community problems or needs. Sunnyvale's assessment includes data on past years and projected or planned indicator levels for the budget year and the year thereafter. An excerpt from this assessment is shown in exhibit 7–1.

In Sunnyvale, this broad perspective of community trends, problems, and needs is a key input in developing the annual budget and management plan. Goals are set which are expressions of the impact the government wants to achieve with respect to a particular community condition. The community condition indicators then provide an objective basis for assessing progress from year to year.

In addition to the broad statement of problems and needs that the community indicators represent, it is also important to identify specific problems in service delivery. Citizen complaints can provide insights on unmet needs. Often, operating agencies are able to pinpoint service delivery problems and other inadequacies. Survey techniques (for example, questioning a sample of citizens each year on how they perceive conditions) are gaining in popularity as a means of assessing needs. Most local programs use a combination of systematic evaluation and *ad hoc* knowledge of problems and opportunities.

Formulating Goals

Goals are broad community aims concerned with major social and environmental concerns—the quality of life. For example, each year, the elected leadership of the city of Dallas, Texas, sets "Goals for Dallas" as a framework for developing and evaluating programs within the city government.

These goals are statements of purpose and direction toward which public resources of the community are to be directed. They provide the policy context within which operational objectives can be developed. Goals may be set in specific legislative enactments, by the state legislature or the local council, or in the local government's charter.

EXHIBIT 7-1

REPRESENTATIVE COMMUNITY CONDITION INDICATORS: CITY OF
SUNNYVALE, CALIFORNIA

1. Transportation

	FY 1969–70	FY 1974–75	Estimated FY 1978–79	Projected FY 1979–80
Citizen Traffic Complaints	280	250	225	210
Traffic Accidents	1,353	2,071	2,650	2,700
Vehicle Miles	9.96	8.54	7.66	7.35
Lane Miles of City-Owned Streets	572	581	590	601

2. Community Development

	FY 1969–70	FY 1974–75	Estimated FY 1978–79	Projected FY 1979–80
Dwelling Units: Single Family	18,999	20,606	21,294	21,521
Multi-Family	10,462	16,252	17,361	17,752
Mobile Homes	2,035	3,486	4,116	4,116
Dwelling Units Needing Minor Repair	4,207	4,234	8,000	8,000
Dwelling Units Needing Major Repair	1,037	1,037	11,000	11,000
Building Safety Permits Issued	4,894	4,365	6,218	7,739

3. Socioeconomic

	FY 1969–70	FY 1974–75	Estimated FY 1978–79	Projected FY 1979–80
City Population	95,408	102,154	106,643	107,189
Jobs in the City	57,138	73,940	88,194	94,000
Unemployed City Residents	2,227	3,890	3,764	3,800
Percent High School Dropouts 16–21 Years Old	8.9%	8.8%	7.4%	6.0%

The process of establishing goals often starts with tentative statements prepared by operating departments with help from budget and management staff, at least the first time around. These drafts may undergo several revisions and refinements during the annual program planning and budgeting cycle.

A common approach is to start broadly and then focus on specifics. This is the case, for example, in Hartford, Connecticut, which has a multilevel series of goals (see exhibit 7–2). Beginning with broad organizational goals, Hartford sets functional, departmental, and finally specific program goals. As the exhibit shows, none of these goals is initially stated in quantitative terms. Only when the goals are translated into objectives and targets are they expressed numerically.

Dayton, Ohio, provides another illustration. Dayton's goals are directly related to citizen perceptions of traffic noise problems, housing conditions, stray dogs, weed conditions, rodent problems, and other neighborhood conditions (see exhibit 7–3). An annual sample survey, which has been repeated now for a decade, is the basis for Dayton's goal setting. So, too, is input from the six highly organized, locally elected Priority Boards that represent Dayton's neighborhoods.

Setting Objectives and Performance Targets

There is little agreement on how to use terms such as goals, objectives, targets, and performance criteria. Goals and objectives are at times used interchangeably. Objectives, targets, and performance criteria all usually involve specific, quantified organizational aims. In this discussion, we'll use these words as follows:

- *Goals* are broad statements of desirable community conditions or program impacts. They are not necessarily quantified, and may describe long-term aims.
- *Objectives* are specific, measurable planned achievements. They may relate to efficiency, service quality, or program effectiveness.
- *Targets* are objectives or any other kind of measurable performance criteria which have specific time frames set for their accomplishment.

Objectives and targets differ from goals because they're more specific and quantifiable so that you know if and when they have been achieved. Operational objectives attempt to translate community goals into operational reality. To be useful, these should be meaningful reflections of specific work efforts. For example, a welfare department's objectives might include maintaining case load error rates at less than 5 percent and completing each case opening or closing within 3 days.

EXHIBIT 7–2
GOALS, OBJECTIVES, AND BUDGET LINKAGES: CITY OF HARTFORD

Health Department

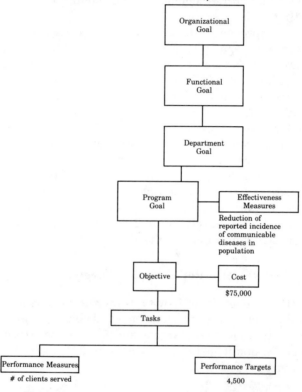

Organizational Goal

The city administration will ensure that within available resources, services will be provided that protect the safety of citizens and neighborhoods of the city and support the policies of the city charter and city council.

Functional Goal

The human resources function will ensure the integrated delivery of social, health, recreational, equal opportunity, and employment services to the citizens of Hartford.

Department Goal

The health department will prevent illness, improve the physical and mental health of citizens, and control environmental hazards.

Program Goal

The Medical and nursing services program will provide preventive and curative health services to adults in order to reduce the incidence of illness.

Objective

The deputy director of health will provide, by contract with Mt. Sinai Hospital, investigative and curative services to 4,500 clients potentially infected with sexually transmitted disease during the fiscal year at a cost of $75,000.

Tasks

Diagnose and treat clients for sexually transmitted diseases

EXHIBIT 7–3
BUDGET POLICIES AND PERFORMANCE TARGETS: CITY OF DAYTON

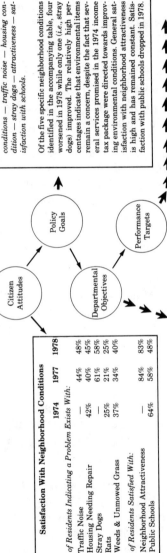

Satisfaction With Neighborhood Conditions

	1974	1977	1978
% of Residents Indicating a Problem Exists With:			
Traffic Noise	—	44%	48%
Housing Needing Repair	42%	40%	45%
Stray Dogs	—	61%	58%
Rats	25%	21%	25%
Weeds & Unmowed Grass	37%	34%	40%
% of Residents Satisfied With:			
Neighborhood Attractiveness	—	84%	83%
Public Schools	64%	58%	48%

9) *Increase satisfaction with neighborhood conditions — traffic noise — housing condition — stray dogs — attractiveness — satisfaction with schools.*

Of the five specific neighborhood conditions identified in the accompanying table, four worsened in 1978 while only one (*i.e.*, stray dogs) improved. The relatively high percentages indicate that environmental items remain a concern, despite the fact that several services promised in the 1974 income tax package were directed towards improving environmental conditions. General satisfaction with neighborhood attractiveness is high and has remained constant. Satisfaction with public schools dropped in 1978.

Objectives

Housing Conservation

Rodent and Weed Control

11.* To implement a weed control program by 5/79 which will mow not less than 750 acres of weeds in 1979.

12.* To conduct a concentrated rodent control program in neighborhoods of medium to heavy infestation as well as isolated problem areas.

13.* To respond to 90% of all rodent and weed complaints within 2 days and 10% within 3 days.

14.* To close 90% of all rodent and weed cases received in 1979.

Performance Criteria	78 3rd Qtr Actual	1979 Estimate
11a. Date program implemented	—	5/79
b. Number of acres mowed	491	750
c. Number of private and urban renewal parcels mowed	1525	2000
12a. Date contract awarded	—	12/78
b. Number of manholes treated	0	2000
c. Number of vacant structures treated	205	600
d. Number of private residences treated	4133	6500
13a. Number of complaints	6276	8700
b. Percent responded to within 2 days.	100%	90%
c. Percent responded to within 3 days.	100%	10%
14a. Number of weed cases received.	1646	2050
b. Percent of weed cases closed.	91%	90%
c. Number of rodent cases received.	4630	7000
d. Percent of rodent cases closed.	99%	90%

If operational objectives are vague (for example, "safe streets"), it's hard to hold an agency accountable. Real accountability is difficult without measurable results-oriented objectives.

The San Diego, California, Fire Department has set a series of specific objectives against which performance is measured and reported periodically to city management. The following two examples show how specific, quantifiable objectives are being used.

Objective: Limit fire deaths and injuries to 20 per 100,000 population.

Objective: Process and complete all fire hazard complaints received from the public within 30 days.

If explicit objectives are set for performance, chief executives and legislators can hold agency heads accountable for how well they use public funds, not just whether they adhere to their budgets. Similarly, agency heads are given an effective tool to use in holding their subordinates accountable and for comparing performance among several operating units with similar responsibilities.

Exhibit 7–3 shows how Dayton translated part of its policy goal regarding neighborhood conditions into well-defined objectives for rodent and weed control. In doing this, Dayton determined what specific activities from a wide range of choices would be used to accomplish each objective. For example, the city decided to implement a new mowing program to control weeds, and selected several specific performance criteria, or targets, to measure progress.

Performance targets should be set at levels that will require more effort than just "business as usual" but that are realistic enough so that they can be achieved consistently and within available resources. Targets that are too easy generate no energy toward improvement. Targets that can't be reached cause managers and workers alike to ignore them.

There are several possible approaches one might employ in arriving at a target. Some of the most common are

- Comparing the current level of achievement with performance in comparable localities
- Negotiations between central managers (such as the manager, mayor, or budget director) and responsible program managers
- Conducting operations and/or program analyses to determine whether there are shortfalls in performance and how great they are

Interjurisdictional Comparisons.   Knowledge about the practices and accomplishments of other localities can provide useful insights to local officials attempting to improve performance. Even simple statistical comparisons of data such as annual cost per household for trash collection, per capita expenditures for parks and recreation, or square miles served per fire station are often helpful.

Negotiating Performance Targets.   In some local governments, targets are negotiated between the chief executive and agency heads, usually during the course of budget formulation. Initial recommendations from the budget staff often argue for target levels several notches above current performance.

Agency heads and their staffs will typically respond that the budget staff's targets are wildly unrealistic and will present their own (which may be well within their ability to deliver).

The chief executive must exercise judgment and diplomacy in working out a compromise. The process is not, however, one that should be left wholly to be decided on the basis of who argues loudest. Experience in prior years, comparisons with what's been achieved in other cities, and as much analysis as can be brought to bear should assist the chief executive in making his decision on the merits.

Operations or Program Analysis.   The more factual knowledge people have about operating problems, shortcomings and current results, the better they're able to set realistic, attainable targets for improvement. For instance, you may know the average time it takes to respond to citizen complaints or requests for service, but this information alone probably won't tell you how to shorten the response time, or how much it can be cut. To do this may require an analysis of the steps involved to find out causes of delay.

Jurisdictions using systematic operations and program analysis techniques often achieve significant gains in performance. Unfortunately, this is an expensive process and must usually be applied selectively.

Methods analysis and work measurement have been used successfully by many jurisdictions. Phoenix, Arizona, has been one of the leaders in applying work measurement to a municipal work force. Work standards have been developed for three-fifths of the work force, saving several million dollars each year through improved efficiency.

The rationality of the planning and budgeting process can be upgraded considerably when there is a firm foundation of commonly agreed-on facts (usually called work standards) as to how many units of work each budgeted position should produce. Policy trade-offs can then be made on the basis of units of output (such as the number of housing inspections to be made) rather than solely on the number of staff positions to be funded.

Preparing Action Plans.   The final step in the "top down" approach to performance accountability is the preparation of a specific action plan.

This is discussed in the final section of this chapter following the review of measurement practices.

What to Measure

Measurement and reporting of performance data serve three different purposes:

- *Assessing performance against targets.* This is feasible only for those programs where outcomes are, in fact, determined largely by managerial performance.
- *Monitoring actual results.* This is what must be done in situations where you can forecast what service levels should be required—but where changes beyond your control may change the situation. For example, in the case of the public assistance or medicaid, the number of eligible people who must be served is beyond a manager's power to control.
- *Building an information base.* This is a useful starting point for programs where current knowledge is not adequate for target setting.

It is important to distinguish among the three purposes because the usefulness of the data depends on how closely they meet their intended purpose. Failure to establish purpose has led some local governments to create elaborate measurement systems that generate masses of data with little apparent impact on program management. Similarly, some budgets and plans fail to distinguish between management objectives and targets, on the one hand, and projections of factors that no manager can control.

Dimensions of Performance Measurement

Now let's turn our attention to the kinds of performance characteristics which can be used in target setting and in measuring and monitoring governmental performance. Essentially, there are three major dimensions:

- *Efficiency* measures performance in the use of resources.
- *Quality of service* captures the variation in the characteristics of service that are not reflected in quantitative measures of output.
- *Program effectiveness* measures progress toward achieving goals.

These dimensions of performance measurement are portrayed schematically in exhibit 7–4. All of these measures have considerable significance and utility to public policy makers and administrators.

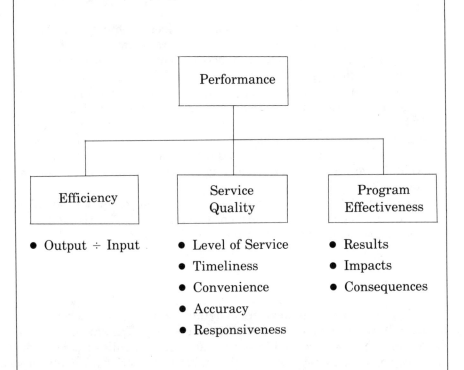

EXHIBIT 7–4

MAJOR DIMENSIONS OF PERFORMANCE MEASUREMENT

Performance

| Efficiency | Service Quality | Program Effectiveness |

- Output ÷ Input
- Level of Service
- Results
- Timeliness
- Impacts
- Convenience
- Consequences
- Accuracy
- Responsiveness

SOURCE: Brian Usilaner and Edwin Soniat. "Productivity Measurement." In *Productivity Improvement Handbook for State and Local Government*, George J. Washnis, Editor. New York, 1979, p. 93.

Efficiency is not measured directly but is, rather, the ratio of output to input. Hence, the following discussion covers the measurement of four variables: input, output, service quality, and program effectiveness.

Input Measures

The most comprehensive measures of input are total program costs or direct program costs. Such cost data are very useful for performance analysis, but they have serious limitations. For example, multi-year or interjurisdictional comparisons cannot be made without adjusting cost data for differences in the general price structure or in wage and salary scales.

As a result, program inputs are frequently measured in terms of man-years, man-hours or man-days of labor input. Manpower usage is a good measure of input in the typically labor-intensive local government. Its principal shortcoming is that it omits capital equipment costs; this is significant because gains in labor productivity are often achieved by investment in labor-saving equipment which increases capital costs.

Both cost and manpower measures involve a practical problem: few local governments require time reporting of work assignments by members of their work force. This creates difficulties in any case where an individual's work time is divided among two or more different programs or work sites.

One may wish to include data on the consumption of some key nonlabor inputs in the reporting of performance information. The rising cost of energy has, for example, drawn attention to the consumption of fuel and electricity and the possibility of conservation.

Output Measures

Selecting the appropriate measure of output for some public services can be difficult. Consider the function of street cleaning. The amount of work done could be measured by the surface area or curb-miles cleaned. The efficiency of a mechanical broom vehicle, however, varies inversely with the speed of operation; beyond about five miles per hour, the faster it travels, the less efficiently it cleans the street. Hence, the measure of the area or distance "cleaned" would have to be accompanied by a quality measure to be of much use. Alternately, the volume or weight of refuse collected might be used, but it is generally impractical to do so.

Street patching—to fill potholes or eliminate broken surfaces—provides another illustration of the difficulties in measuring output. The number of tons of patching material laid down is the most readily available and commonly used measure. However, this produces the danger that work crews might be wasteful in use of expensive materials. Thus, how the material is used as well as the amount used must be carefully monitored.

In a significant proportion of the programs and activities of local government, there is no single, unambiguous measurable output. For example, in the course of a single shift, a police patrol may engage in different activities, such as random patrol; response to radio calls; issuance of traffic tickets; issuance of parking tickets; making arrests; checking closed business premises; investigation of previously reported crimes; serving of summons and warrants; investigation of suspicious situations and persons; and making out crime reports. All of these activities are measurable and all are necessary for any analysis of performance—but there is no single measure of output from which patrol efficiency can be determined.

Service Quality

Factory products can be seen, felt, measured and tested; services cannot. They are consumed immediately and nothing but the satisfaction remains to be measured. Even so, certain attributes of service quality can be described. These include timeliness, responsiveness, thoroughness, accuracy, courtesy, and respect. Many citizen complaints involve issues of quality such as the timeliness with which a service is provided; the helpfulness shown by government employees; or the accuracy of the work done. Some quality characteristics can be measured objectively (for example, error rates, response times) while others rely on subjective consumer perceptions (for example, safe streets or well-kept parks).

If the amount of service produced per unit of labor is used to measure relative efficiency, the quality of service also must be monitored to assure consistency. Otherwise, what may appear to be a change in efficiency may really be the result of a change in quality. A difference in response time, for example, between two fire departments could be the result of a difference in resources (such as the number of fire stations and fire companies). Unless this quality characteristic is considered, the department with the slowest response would appear to be the most productive even though its fire suppression capability is much less. These two fire departments are providing different products which are defined by their respective service quality characteristics.

Some service quality differences grow out of the basic design of the program. Interjurisdictional comparisons of refuse collection productivity, for example, are commonly made on the basis of tons collected per man-day. This is a good but rough measure only if, in fact, the local governments compared are providing the same service. Refuse is most commonly collected at the curb or along alleys but in some jurisdictions refuse collectors pick up from refuse containers in back yards, garages, or even cellars. Obviously, collection tonnage per man-day tends to be lower where this extra service is available.

Program Effectiveness

Program effectiveness measures the impact of a program on its intended target(s). It can be measured by comparing observed results to one or more of the following: a similar target population not served by the program; the situation before the program began; some ideal situation such as absence of poverty or malnutrition; or an administratively established goal.

Program objectives are first defined and then measures selected to evaluate results. Subtle differences in the way measures are defined can have a strong influence on how effective a program is shown to be. Because of the difficulty and expense involved in collecting involved in program evaluation data, partial or surrogate measures may be used.

Significant problems arise when we try to measure program impact. Some of the most widely used measures of governmental performance have serious shortcomings. An example is crime statistics. Does an increase in reported crime mean that criminals are more active or that the police are encouraging more citizens to report crime? The wider attention in recent years to the crime of rape has almost certainly been a factor in increasing the number of rapes reported. Similarly, changes in the number of arrests may reflect changes in police policy as much as in police activities; for example, in cases where the police decide to concentrate on serious felonies, total arrests may decline.

Program effectiveness is almost always more complex and difficult to measure than is program efficiency. In many programs, effectiveness can be determined only through special evaluation studies. This is especially true of education and training programs. Counseling and health care are also difficult to evaluate in terms of effectiveness.

In most programs, however, some data bearing on effectiveness can be gathered routinely. For example, drop-out ratios, attendance data, and job placement rates are all only partial indicators of the effectiveness of job training programs, but they can be easily collected and reported and provide at least some important hints about program value.

The Urban Institute has given considerable attention to the development of measures of effectiveness for local government programs. Anyone who wants to start a local measurement program focused on effectiveness would do well by reading the Institute's publications first (see the Bibliography at the end of this volume for citations).

Process Descriptors

In the foregoing paragraphs we have identified three categories of data which can inform local government officials about significant aspects of governmental performance. They encompass the concepts of efficiency, quality of service, and program effectiveness or impact. There is also a fourth body of information which, while not always incorporated within the scope of performance management systems, is nevertheless of fundamental importance in evaluating and improving service performance. We call these "process descriptors."

Process descriptors provide information about the nature and workings of the processes which are used to convert resources (inputs) into services (outputs). They include data about demands for service, work backlogs, processing cycles, crew sizes, and worker performance.

Information about service demand characteristics provides crucial input to decisions about how, where, and when to deploy productive resources. For example, the locations of fire stations and fire company manning schedules relative to the timing and dispersion of fire incidence have a direct bearing on response time.

Monitoring work backlogs can provide an early warning of production bottlenecks. Processing cycles can directly impact on service responsiveness. If it seems to take forever for your government to respond to citizen requests or complaints, you may find the problem to be a consequence of large backlogs, an excessive number of sequential processing steps, or both.

Finally, it should be self-evident that excessive crew sizes in relation to the tasks to be performed (often found in street patching operations) and poor work performance both contribute directly to low efficiency.

Process descriptors hold the greatest meaning and utility to line managers who are charged with managing, monitoring, and controlling day-to-day operations.

Choosing Measures

The choice of what measures to use is likely to be based, in most cases, on what it is possible to measure rather than on any ideal about what ought to be measured. The relatively few localities that have organized comprehensive, multiagency performance measurement systems have done so only after a period of experience concentrated in one or two agencies. As they proceed toward defining goals and objectives, these jurisdictions are likely to find initial measures inadequate, in part because the goal-setting process focuses more on program objectives and program performance and less on operational concerns such as quantity and efficiency of the production process. Thus, attention moves toward methods of acquiring new kinds of information involving more expensive sources such as citizen surveys, trained observers, and new information systems.

The city of Charlotte, North Carolina, has a management-by-objectives program which has evolved much along the lines we just described (see exhibit 7–5).

The Costs of Measurement

Performance management systems that start with measurement systems often base their first efforts on readily available data sources which require little effort and cost. These are likely to include output quantities and some key quality measures such as response time, error rates, and complaints. These data elements are "by-product" measures—information that is produced as a direct result of service delivery. For example, when the police communications unit records the time of a citizen's request for help and the time the patrol car is dispatched to the scene, it is doing more than just keeping records. It is also producing a basis for response time measurement. When the public works department's administrative clerk records each day the workers who show up on time, those who are late, and those who are out sick, the record is important for payroll and other administrative purposes—but it is also useful for measuring employee performance.

Reliance on these internally generated performance data need not be a serious constraint. The Memphis/Shelby County, Tennessee, Library system, for example, has developed a variety of meaningful performance measures from internal records (see exhibit 7–6).

By-product data have two features which are particularly pleasing to municipal managers. They cost less to aggregate and are likely to be reasonably accurate because they are part of a formal administrative record that the public agency needs for internal operating purposes.

Where by-product data are not available, it is necessary to set up systems to gather data on either a one-time or continuing basis. Most performance measurement systems ultimately rely to some degree on special data gathering despite its cost and the difficulties of getting accurate data. Some representative costs of data acquired through the use of trained observers and survey instruments are shown in exhibit 7–7.

Cost tends to be proportional to the frequency of the data collection effort. Before you set up an external data collection system to obtain information more often than once or twice per year, you should be sure there is a real need for it.

EXHIBIT 7-5

EVOLUTION OF PERFORMANCE ACCOUNTABILITY: CITY OF CHARLOTTE, N.C.

Performance indices in the first program budget (FY 1973) contained a preponderance of workload measures; that is, quantities of work done such as number of fire alarm responses, tons of solid waste collected, and buildings inspected.

Charlotte moved quickly toward measures which were meaningful in evaluating program efficiency and effectiveness. Thus, in the following year, FY 1974, when greater emphasis was placed on improving productivity, many of the work objectives were aimed at increasing the amount of work done per dollar or per man-year expended. Initial attempts were made also to set targets in terms of response time to calls for service or length of time to complete specific actions.

Objectives relating to service quality, such as the condition of street surfaces, began to be addressed in FY 1975 and gained increasing attention in FY 1976. These advancements were not easy. As the year-end report for FY 1974 states:

> Some of the objectives proved difficult to measure because of the inadequate data, and a few objectives proved to be unrealistic.

Another continuing problem was to state objectives in terms specific enough to be useful from a managerial standpoint. Recognizing that more elaborate data collection procedures are needed as objectives become clearer, Charlotte is developing data-capturing mechanisms which will enable the effectiveness of their efforts to be assessed better. For instance, rating systems have been developed to measure service quality of street cleaning, landscaping, and street maintenance.

The direction and extent of the progress made by the MBO program can be illustrated by comparing statements for law enforcement for FY 1972 and FY 1976. In 1972, the entire statement consisted of the following:

> The principal function of the Police Department is to preserve the peace and protect the life and property of the Community and its citizens.

In contrast, the 1976 program budget for law enforcement is quite lengthy and rich in descriptive details and quantitative objectives. For instance, even while recognizing the severe limitations inherent in present approaches to measuring law enforcement services, Charlotte nevertheless includes specific targets for crime deterrence; for example, "Hold auto thefts to 5.1 or fewer incidents per 1,000 population."

One unusual aspect of the Charlotte program is the inclusion as formal objectives of time commitments to develop new information systems. Perhaps an illustration will make this point clear. One long-term objective of traffic engineering is to ensure that painted traffic control markers are highly visible. This objective was specified quantitatively on the basis of a visibility rating system which had not yet been implemented because two intermediate tasks were required to make the objective operational. Consequently, the FY 1976 goal was to comlete the task, which consisted of:

- Developing a simple rating method to measure paint marking deteriorations, and
- Developing a monitoring system to periodically check paint markings and tie this system into the paint crew work scheduling systems.

In this way, Charlotte's MBO program has incorporated targets to improve the governmental processes as preliminary steps toward improving the results.

Annual budget proposals submitted to the council are accompanied by a message from the City Manager which presents the budget's financial implications and summarizes accomplishments and commitments. The tone of these messages since MBO was initiated has been conservative in claiming accomplishments. Promises of future improvements also are made carefully and in language that imparts a feeling of objectivity and credibility. Early on, the MBO effort was thought to be a five-year developmental process. It is clear now that the process has no definitive end point because expectations continue to rise as advancements are made, thus constituting a continual press foward in the "state-of-the-art" of managing municipal services.

Service delivery in Charlotte has improved since the MBO program was started. Crews for solid waste collection were reduced from four men to three in 1974, saving the city $200,000 per year. Also, a new computerized fire reporting system has been installed which, coupled with a more aggressive, problem-oriented fire inspection effort, has contributed to a 29 percent decline in fires in inspected occupancies during the last six months of 1975.

Although it is readily acknowledged that some improvements may have occurred had there been no MBO program, there appears to have been a significant impact. Attitudes are changing and new managerial styles are evolving, as evidenced by the following:

- The Traffic Department has revised methods of handling citizen requests to achieve more timely responses.
- The Police Department is cooperating with the Office of Budget and Evaluation in an analysis of its patrol function.
- The Fire Department is measuring and exploring alternatives to achieve an optimum response time.
- New techniques are being used to evaluate effectiveness of street repair, cleaning, and landscaping.

SOURCE: *Improving Governmental Productivity: Selected Case Studies.* Spring 1977. National Center for Productivity and Quality of Working Life. Washington, D.C., p. 23.

EXHIBIT 7–6

PERFORMANCE MEASUREMENT:
MEMPHIS—SHELBY COUNTY LIBRARY

The Memphis/Shelby County Library has an extensive program of performance measures that include output measures, efficiency measures, and effectiveness measures. Their output measures include

• Number of items circulated for home use
• Number of reference and information inquiries
• Number of persons reached with programs
• Number of items processed for patrons' use
• Number of registered borrowers.

Efficiency measures currently in use are

• Cost per item circulated
• Cost per capita for circulated items
• Number of items circulated per staff member
• Cost per reference inquiry
• Cost per capita for reference inquiries
• Number of inquiries per staff
• Cost per person reached with programs
• Cost per item processed

The effectiveness measures used by the library are

• The number of items circulated per capita
• Percent of titles requested not owned
• Average waiting time for reserved books
• Number of reference inquiries handled per capita and per staff member
• Percent of ALA standards reached for book acquisitions
• Percent of reference inquiries staff could not answer
• Percent of population reached by programs
• Number of items processed per capita

In addition to the above measures, the Memphis Library has a group of performance measures that are routinely reported as part of their budget request. The development and acceptance of the budgetary performance measures for the library are still in formative stages since quantitative measures are relatively new to the city budgeting system. In addition to the specific objective and performance measures established in the budget, the Memphis Library also has a set of overall objectives that prioritize the functions (information function, education function, cultural function, and recreational function) to be served by the library as well as explicitly prioritizing the major clientele groups (adults, young adults, children, and educationally and economically disadvantaged).

SOURCE: *Effectiveness Measures: Literature and Practice Review*. U.S. Department of Housing and Urban Development. Washington, D.C., 1979, p. 47.

EXHIBIT 7–7

REPRESENTATIVE COSTS OF ACQUIRING EFFECTIVENESS DATA

Function	Type of Data Collected	Method Employed	Frequency	Estimated Annual Costs*
Waste Collection	Street Cleanliness	Sampling by Trained Observer	2 Times/Year	$7,500 to $20,000
Recreation	Citizen and User Perceptions Physical Conditions of Facilities	Sampling Surveys Trained Observer	1 Time/Year Seasonal	$15,000 to $30,000
Library	User Perceptions Selected In-Library Activities	User Survey Internal Data Collection	1 Time/Year	$7,000 (4 library system)
Crime Control	Citizen Perceptions	Citizen Survey	1 Time/Year	$3,000 to $15,000

SOURCE: Harry Hatry et al. *How Effective Are Your Community Services?* The Urban Institute and the International City Management Association. Washington, D.C. 1977.

*Costs are in 1976 dollars and should be increased by a factor sufficient to cover inflation since that year.

Organizing and Operating the System

How should a local government organize to carry out a performance accountability program? There are a number of options, any of which can prove effective. The specific choice is likely to be influenced by the existing structure of local government and who is willing to take the initiative in getting a program off the ground.

Initiative and Central Direction

In the most successful local performance management systems, the initiative has been taken by the chief executive. In a small number of cases, the city council or local legislature has provided the initial thrust.

Usually, the program's direction has been centralized, either in the immediate office of the chief executive, in the central budget office, or in a special staff set up for the purpose. Milwaukee, Wisconsin, a city which has one of the longest continuing performance measurement efforts in the nation, elected to assign the responsibility to the central budget agency. In other municipalities, where the budget agency is disinclined to broaden its functions and responsibilities, a central management improvement or operations office, if one exists, might be the best choice.

Operating Agency Participation

For effective management to spread throughout local government, it is also essential to enlist the participation of the heads of the operating agencies and their principal staff and line units. In fact, quite effective programs have been mounted within the operating departments of local government.

The process can be initiated in a single agency in response to a situation that is perceived to involve an actual or incipient breakdown of customary managerial and administrative processes. For example, there may be an accelerating trend in fire alarms that threatens the stability of existing response systems. Another example might involve rapid deterioration and abandonment of the housing stock in a particular neighborhood.

Characteristically, performance improvement efforts that start in a single agency are later found to have potential application in other agencies. This process of evolution—successful implementation on a small scale while staff capabilities and techniques develop—is then followed by expansion to other agencies.

Responsibility Centers

Performance accountability should not stop with the heads of agencies. It's also important to involve the officials directly responsible for the administration of specific programs and activities. Performance accountability should, in this respect, parallel the pattern of fiscal accountability. Basic responsibility for performance as well as finances should be placed on the heads of the major operating units designated as responsibility centers. These managers, in turn, should establish similar objectives for their subordinates where the scale and organization of the responsibility center make this necessary.

The Integrated Approach

Perhaps the most effective combination of central overhead and line agency interactions comes about when the central staff develops the planning framework and then provides back-up and specialist support to line agencies. Effective line agency operations in turn need strong commitment from the department head and internal staff support in the form of analysts and engineers to assist in planning, implementing, and measuring the outcomes of improvement efforts. For a fully effective performance management program, the central and line functions both need to be present and their activities have to be integrated into a single system.

Useful Starting Points

Whether the program is to be governmentwide or not, some functions are better starting points than others. The reasons for omitting some agencies, at least initially, may be a realistic appraisal of the political facts of life or of the greater difficulties involved in mounting efforts in some agencies than in others. Studies of the most effective municipal productivity efforts suggest that key targets of opportunity for measurable service improvement have been found more often in agencies that deliver visible and measurable services (such as sanitation and highways) than in those where service outputs are harder to measure and which often tend to have considerable political independence (such as police and education).

Linking Management to the Budget

The performance management program should eventually, if not initially, be integrated into regular government operations by tying it to the budget cycle. Policy guidance can then include the chief executive's instructions on management and service goals as well as on expenditure constraints. Agency expenditure estimates can be required to include measures of performance such as workload levels as well as efficiency improvement targets, output expansion, and quality improvements. The dollar figures in the executive budget can be accompanied by comparable target data on performance to explain to the local legislature and the citizenry what the budget will "buy"—as well as what it will pay for. The process should not stop with budget adoption but should go on throughout the year, making possible periodic review by both agency heads and the chief executive of how well the locality is doing with respect to its management as well as its fiscal targets.

Performance accountability cannot be effectively linked to fiscal accountability unless performance measures and fiscal data are reported for the same program and organizational groupings. Unless the same groupings are used, it is impossible to determine efficiency or cost-effectiveness from regularly reported data.

Preparing Plans and Achieving Action

There are a number of techniques that localities have found useful in converting their performance objectives into operational steps to achieve better results in public service delivery. The most important of these are discussed next. They include action plans based on timetables; an overall management plan; and reporting systems which spell out whether the desired performance is being achieved.

Action Plans and Timetables.   Objectives become operational when they're converted into action plans that establish the means by which targets are to be achieved. Action plans reduce the risks that once the program budget is adopted, managerial attention may be diverted and the momentum lost.

Action plans express how and when objectives are to be accomplished. Although such plans take many forms, project management techniques are often employed. Common ingredients of such plans, as shown in exhibit 7–8 from Phoenix, Arizona, are

- A list of steps required
- A specific date for completing each step
- Identification of the organization and sometimes the individual responsible for each step

A detailed, step-by-step action plan is most important when achieving the specified objective depends on actions by more than one agency or organization, involves a large number of sequential or concurrent steps, or requires significant changes in procedures and work processes. The action plan is the means of managing the improvement process.

The Management Plan.   An advanced concept used in some localities to integrate their performance accountability systems is the idea of the

EXHIBIT 7–8

PERFORMANCE ACHIEVEMENT PROGRAM:
ACTION PLAN, CITY OF PHOENIX

77–78		Director of Livestock Services	5/1/78
FY	NAME	POSITION	DATE

City of Phoenix	**performance achievement program** **ACTION PLAN**

Result Areas	Performance Indicators	Action Plan		What Preparatory Action is Needed
		What Will Be Done	When	
1. Sanitation	a. Program deficiencies	• Review federal standards with division heads	6/1/78	• Obtain copy of federal regs.
		• Conduct in-house inspection using federal rules	8/1/78	
	b. Animals destroyed	• Identify specific sanitary problems which can lead to death of animals	7/15/78	• Assign _____ to do thorough study
		• Determine how these specific problems can be overcome	8/15/78	
		• Instruct inspectors to concentrate on prevention measures	9/1/78	
	c. Federal citations to livestock owners	• Write a pamphlet explaining federal regs. in layman's language	10/20/78	• Assign _____ to this
		• Obtain federal approval for pamphlet	1/15/79	

management plan. In its most fully developed form, the management plan sets forth agency missions and programmatic objectives together with a statement of the resources, performance levels, and action plans describing how each objective will be achieved. This is not an unreachable state for municipal government. Cities of very different sizes including New York City and St. Petersburg, Florida, have adopted such plans. In these municipalities, interested civic and neighborhood groups can become informed about the progress of government administration through specific measures, not just press releases.

Management Reporting Systems. Inherent in the concept of a performance-oriented management system are three component elements:*

- The objective to be achieved
- The measures to be used to monitor progress in reaching the objective
- Periodic reports on progress

Communities where progressive management systems are in place commonly address these three elements through the following types of documents:

- The *budget* is the place where the objectives are initially stated. Good budgetary practice also calls for measures of performance in achieving objectives to be stated in the budget.
- *Periodic progress reports* describe levels of accomplishment related to each objective. Good systems usually call for internal progress reports once a month and public progress reports on a less frequent basis.
- *Annual year-end management reports* summarize accomplishments and explain which objectives were accomplished, which were not, and the reasons for the shortfalls (sometimes called variance reports). An annual management report is a useful "report card" on how well municipal managers are doing, compared both to one another and to the targets that were assigned to them.

Reporting techniques used in these three documents are similar, although there is often a tendency to focus in the budget on items that can be measured in dollars while progress reports and the management plan also frequently cover nonfiscal matters such as improvements in civil service systems and other personnel-related subjects.

Two types of reporting techniques are commonly used:

- A comparison of current performance levels against a "plan" or "tar-

---

*In a really advanced system, an audit or evaluation component would also be included for after-the-fact examination of what the program achieved.

get." The target can be divided into monthly or quarterly units so that the most recent rate of accomplishment can be seen as well as year-to-date performance as illustrated in exhibit 7–9.
- Measurement of progress against "milestones." This involves an initial planning process which develops a sequential schedule of events that have to be accomplished. Each major event is termed a "milestone" and progress can be measured in terms of the number or percent of milestones reached in a given time period as compared to the number scheduled in the plan for the same elapsed time period.

Accountability should permeate the operation of municipal agencies. Rather than merely measuring overall performance, the system should be extended to the lowest level of responsibility feasible. In most cases, this is the lowest level at which there is a clear supervisory responsibility over a function. Thus, there should be targets and performance reports not only for the sanitation or parks department as a whole but also for the significant units within these agencies such as service delivery districts, the unit responsible for vehicle maintenance and repairs, and major staff support units.

A hierarchical series of reports can be produced so that each successive managerial level need review only those matters and measures that have the greatest relevance. Thus, the district level supervisor obviously needs data on his own unit's performance and also on that of similar units for comparison purposes. The departmental commissioner needs data on his entire agency covering both staff and line functions. The chief executive must have information that covers all agencies under his purview. The legislature needs an overview as well, but usually in less detail. In order to keep the data flow to a manageable level, they should contain fewer measures of increasingly broader significance as they move up the chain of command.

Systematic Approach

Over the long run the most effective municipal management is likely to be that which takes a systematic approach to building the concept of management accountability into its overall operations. Inspired initiatives have their place, but to be truly effective accountability must be built into the on-going pattern of operations of municipal government. The best systems are those which exist in localities where periodic checking of "progress against plan" is an accepted way of life, as it appears to be in Overland Park, Kansas (see Exhibit 7–10).

EXHIBIT 7-9

PRODUCTIVITY PROGRESS REPORT

Productivity Program Progress Report

Agency _____

Program/Function	Unit of Measure	Fy 1972–1973	FY 1973–1974 Target		First Quarter			Second Quarter			Third Quarter			Fourth Quarter			Remarks
					July	Aug.	Sept.	Oct.	Nov.	Dec.	Jan.	Feb.	Mar.	Apr.	May	June	
				M O N T H L Y Target													
				Actual													
				% of Target													
				Y E A R T O D A T E Target													
				Actual													
				% of Target													

Page ____of ____

SOURCE: John S. Thomas. *So, Mr. Mayor, You Want to Improve Productivity.* National Commission on Productivity and Work Quality in Cooperation with the Ford Foundation. Washington, D.C. 1974.

EXHIBIT 7–10
GOVERNMENT BY OBJECTIVES: OVERLAND PARK, KANSAS
Overland Park, Kansas: Governing by Objectives

In OVERLAND PARK, KANSAS (77,000), the approach to goal setting is called GOVERNING BY OBJECTIVES. GBO is a comprehensive approach to planning and goal setting which uses the principles of Management by Objectives (MBO) in all phases of city government. The entire Overland Park government operation has a place in GBO—the governing body, professional and clerical staff, and the citizens.

GBO was started to give the governing body a larger framework for developing policies and give the staff an expanded management systems capacity for carrying out the policies. More simply, GBO means goal setting by the governing body, program budgeting and "MBO" by the staff, participation by the citizens in goal setting and policy making, and training, performance agreements, and performance appraisals for the city staff.

These are the basic elements of GBO:

1. GOVERNING BODY POLICY DEVELOPMENT CAPACITY
   Four major goal areas and Council committees for each area
   Policy objectives set by each committee
   Policy manual for easy reference
   Quarterly reports to citizens
   Council agenda format based on the goal areas

2. PROGRAM POLICY DEVELOPMENT CAPACITY
   Program budget format
   Citizen participation in goal setting
   Program goals and objectives
   Quarterly progress reports by the staff to the governing body
   Annual program evaluation

3. MANAGEMENT SYSTEMS CAPACITY
   Work plans based on goals and objectives
   Supervisor performance agreements
   Employee performance agreements
   Employee appraisal by objectives
   Training and counseling

GBO was born out of a sense of confusion in government—more federal regulations, new state restrictions, increased regional government, new problems, higher expectations, expanded citizen demands, and, in some cases, poor decision making. The program was developed by the staff—not without some reservation, apprehension, and confusion among the elected officials about overhauling the city's longstanding way of doing business.

The program began in December 1974. First, the governing body and staff identified four major goal areas and established standing Council committees for each goal area. A department head was assigned to work with each committee. Those goal areas are FINANCE AND ADMINISTRATION; COMMUNITY DEVELOPMENT; PUBLIC SAFETY; and TRANSPORTATION. They were based on what seemed to be the major concerns in Overland Park at that time. While the goal areas are supposed to be long range, they aren't static. Each year they are

continued

EXHIBIT 7–10 (*continued*)

reexamined to make sure that the areas are still relevant. Within each goal area, functional units of city operation were defined, called "cost centers." For example, under Public Safety, the police department is a major cost center.

Given that basic framework, here's how GBO works:

1. Staff members in each cost center prepare draft goal statements with specific objectives.
2. The staff proposal is submitted to the appropriate committee (police department goals to the Public Safety committee, etc.)
3. The committee reviews and revises the staff goal statement and recommends a goal statement to be adopted by the council for that cost center.
4. Citizens may speak to the proposed goals and objectives BEFORE the staff begins to prepare the budget. Another formal public hearing is held immediately before the budget is adopted.
5. Staff prepares a program budget based on the goals and objectives for each cost center.
6. Staff prepares quarterly reports to the manager and the governing body showing progress on goals—either ahead of schedule, on target, or behind schedule with any appropriate comments. Quarterly progress reports are also prepared for the citizens and mailed to each household in the city.
7. An evaluation system to determine the "cost effectiveness" of each program and to determine priorities for future years is being developed now. In order to emphasize involvement of both the governing body and the public, an evaluation program using citizen task forces and the council goal committees will be used. The task forces and council committees together will evaluate programs with help from the staff and make recommendations to the council before the next budget is prepared.
8. Each goal committee reviews its policy objectives every six months— in January and July. An ACTION PLAN—a tentative policy agenda—is prepared which lists major issues to be discussed during the next six months.

GBO is still in a developing stage, but officials say there have been "dramatic changes in the way we do business." From the governing body's viewpoint, Council members feel they know more about what's going on in the city. They have a better opportunity to think things through before making decisions and admittedly they have to work harder—but they feel they're better equipped to do that work effectively.

Citizen involvement and interest in the process has also been significant. Already a group of business leaders are participating in a pilot task force program to begin the job of evaluating programs.

And, from the employee's viewpoint, city workers on all levels of local government are working more closely with the governing body.

SOURCE: *Goal Setting by the Governing Body: The Why and How.* U.S. Department of Housing and Urban Development, Washington, D.C., p. 21.

Advanced Techniques

Good managers like to keep up with the developing "state of the art" in management practice. Thus, some notes on more advanced approaches may be in order—as long as the reader recognizes that these are only options for use where appropriate.

With the advent of computerized data systems, it has become possible to record and summarize data more speedily and at less cost. The flexibility of a well-designed computer system also makes it possible for a higher level official (such as the chief executive) to focus on a specific, high priority project in more detail than he would normally receive. One systematic way of reporting useful details while not burying higher level officials in volumes of computer printout is to report such details only on a "by exception" basis—when a priority project or activity is running well behind schedule or target level of accomplishments.

New organizational techniques which originated in the private sector have also found useful application in municipal productivity programs as well. Among the most useful techniques have been project scheduling and project management.

Project scheduling is an approach to specifying time targets for the accomplishment of a program objective. The technique also is known under names such as "arrow diagramming," "critical path method" (or CPM), and PERT ("project evaluation and review technique"). In essence, this approach depends on precise scheduling of each sequential activity (or "milestone") needed to achieve a goal. A common use of the method is in programming and construction of capital facilities. A less common but equally effective use is the scheduling of high priority municipal activities that require the closely coordinated participation of several different agencies.

Project management is an organizational approach that has been found highly effective in situations that involve multiple agency participation. It is often utilized in conjunction with project scheduling. Personnel from various agencies are detached from their regular responsibilities to operate under the guidance of a single project manager to whom the responsibility of accomplishing a specific target is assigned. An example of such a project might be an innovative approach to vermin extermination which requires unified participation by local health, housing and sanitation agencies. In such a case, the "project management" approach can enlist personnel from different agencies or chains of command into a single unified team, capable of moving with less bureaucratic delay than is the case with more standardized management approaches where each agency sticks to its own functions and no one accepts overall responsibility. A variant of the project management approach that has been used in industry but rarely in government involves delegation of full authority to the project manager to make all necessary decisions without referring back to the regular management chain of command. In most governmental uses of the technique, agency heads retain their authority but agree to provide needed decisions on an expedited basis.

In some larger municipalities, teams of specialists with experience in project scheduling and management are maintained as part of a central administrative support function in the office of the chief executive. This could also be a function performed by a central division of management or administrative services.

Some Other Aspects of Performance Management

There are many different aspects of local government in which a performance approach is useful. One way of looking at these different aspects is in terms of whether the issue is one of program, personnel, or contract management. We have already discussed the accountability process as it applies to internal programming functions, but a few additional comments on applying the same concepts to personnel and contract management are pertinent.

Personnel management is a critical feature of government because in most cases it is where most public money is spent. In most localities, nearly two in every three municipal dollars go to pay the salaries and related costs of public employees. Personnel managers need to measure the performance they are getting in return for wages.One set of personnel measures has to do with such matters as coming to work on time and taking sick leave only when necessary. Other measures may directly test employee performance, such as the number of building or boiler inspections completed per day per inspector.

Contracts with private organizations are important in many local governments. For example, voluntary child care agencies may recruit and monitor foster families or early childhood education programs may be operated under contract by parochial schools. Some cities obtain sanitation services by private contract, most have buildings built by private construction firms, and a few even contract out police functions (but usually only to other levels of government). One obvious measure of a contract service is the cost, but it is usually a good idea to have other measures of performance as well. For example, does the child care agency meet all of the locality's requirements in assuring foster children prompt placement and a fair opportunity to return to their natural families? Does the private sanitation company pick up refuse in a timely and predictable fashion so that street litter is kept to a minimum? In a growing number of states and localities these measures of performance are being written directly into the contract with periodic reporting requirements to assure the quality of performance.

Summing Up: Achieving Accountability

This chapter has described the key features of performance management. It has tried to advance the concept that performance management is a necessary accountability link in local fiscal management.

Some common elements can be found in successful management accountability programs in local government. They include

- Strong top-management support
- Extensive involvement by agency personnel and other potential data users in the selection and development of measures and targets
- Assignment of sufficient staff to measurement and analysis
- A step-by-step approach, building upon the capabilities and interests of line managers
- Flexibility to change focus and evolve to satisfy changing interests and needs
- Linking measurement to accountability; measurement systems without accountability tend to become sterile and irrelevant.

We believe that performance accountability can best be viewed as a contract between general management and program managers; funds are appropriated for each program on the premise that performance will meet agreed-upon targets and actual performance is monitored to see that it does meet those targets.

This chapter alone won't prepare the reader to design a performance management program. If you want to read more about the subject, the Bibliography at the end of this volume lists other publications that will provide useful insights. You may also want to communicate with your local university, state technical assistance agencies, or your HUD regional office for additional information and assistance.

Integrated Financial Management Information Systems 8

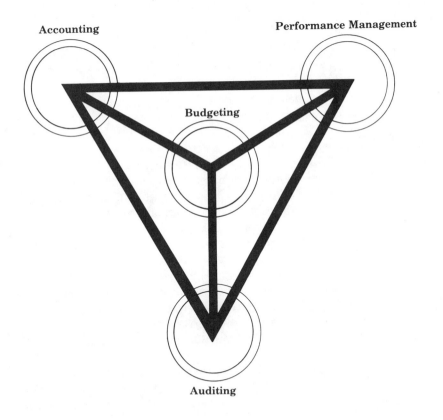

Accounting

Performance Management

Budgeting

Auditing

"Over the next five years, local governments—large and small—will face key decisions"

The financial management information system plays a vital role in the integration of the four financial management functions. Much of the actual linkage between functions actually happens through the flow of data. Indeed, much of the discussion in the preceding chapters on budgeting, accounting, and performance management has been concerned with the need to generate and transmit the information essential to effective local management.

The central characteristic of an integrated financial management information system is the capacity to provide both financial and performance data classified in the many different ways required to serve the various objectives of the four financial management functions. Unfortunately, at present most local governments do not have such fully integrated information systems—a situation that reflects the compartmentalized development of the financial management functions and the cost and difficulty of integrating them.

An increasing number of local governments have been installing integrated information systems. This has been made far easier by advances in computer hardware and software. It is also due, however, to an increased awareness of the deficiencies of traditional accounting information systems, especially in those local governments with serious fiscal problems.

For example, in 1975, in response to severe financial pressures and external demands, the city of New York began a $24 million project to redesign its financial management systems. Central to the effort was the creation of a computerized, integrated financial management information system.

While New York is the largest, it is by no means the only local government with new systems for capturing, processing, and reporting financial and other data. Dayton, Ohio, with funding and other support from the federal Urban Information Systems Inter-Agency Committee spent five years developing a new system. Sunnyvale, California, has developed its own system. Other cities with recently installed systems include Burbank, California; Fort Lauderdale, Florida; San Antonio, Texas; San Francisco, California; Portsmouth, Virginia; Washington, D.C.; and Wethersfield, Connecticut. A growing variety of packaged and specially tailored systems for both small and large local governments are now available.

Many more cities are considering new financial information systems or will do so in the next few years. This chapter focuses on the elements of integrated information systems (in contrast to the more prevalent independent systems), their benefits and costs, and the strategic considerations involved.

Elements of an Integrated Information System

Most existing local financial information systems evolved from rather independent beginnings within the individual financial functions. Accountants set up systems to meet formal reporting requirements; budgeting people established systems for budget planning and control; and operating managers set up their own systems. Definitions and files were usually not consistent from one system to another, and, for most purposes, did not need to be. While each system measured a dimension of organizational performance, they did so from differing perspectives.

In integrated systems, financial (and, sometimes, performance) data are consolidated into a unified data base servicing the separate functions. When successfully accomplished, this avoids duplication in the recording and processing of data, and also provides for timely analyses and controls.

While there are many different approaches, most integrated systems contain the following:

- A unified data base
- Computerized internal edits and controls
- Flexibility for modification and analysis
- Varying levels of operational integration and centralized controls

Each of these characteristics is described here.

Unified Data Base

The collection of management information within a unified data base is conceptually straightforward. Financial transactions (such as receipts, payments, or other steps in the transfer of funds) are recorded at the lowest level of detail, and categorized or coded with respect to all of the characteristics important to users, whether accountants, budget examiners, managers, funding agencies, or others. In a similar fashion, relevant events in the production and delivery of services can also be recorded and categorized. Summaries or higher level reports are assembled by aggregating or "rolling up" the detailed data as needed.

In comparison with systems that focus separately on budgeted appropriations or accounting funds and objects, integrated systems typically require several major changes:

- Consistency in definitions and accounting principles
- Classification of data by program, subprogram, and activity
- Classification by the organizational hierarchy (such as department, division, responsibility center, special project, or neighborhood)
- In some cases, the inclusion of performance data

The concept of an integrated information system is simple but, in practice, it is complicated by the number of government agencies, programs, funds, and funding sources, and, sometimes, by conflicting accounting and reporting requirements. Computers are required to maintain and manipulate the vast amounts of data and detail.

The major advantage of the integrated system is that, once classifications and accounting principles are adequately defined, financial transactions and performance events need be entered only once, with their contribution to each of the relevant classifications measured at that time. The computer can automatically post these values to files maintained for various reporting purposes (see exhibit 8–1). This is called "single transaction processing," or "multiple posting." It avoids some of the costs, delays, and errors that occur when data are passed from unit to unit within the government.

Internal Edits and Controls

Multiple posting can potentially create multiple errors, so error control must be carefully managed. Moreover, under integrated systems clerks must enter more data elements for an individual transaction. For example, where an accounting entry under an independent accounting system might need codes for the fiscal year, appropriation, fund and object of expenditure, the same entry under an integrated system might also require codes for the responsibility center, project, and other attributes. Exhibit 8–2 lists the accounting data elements maintained in one commercially available system.

Integrated systems try to minimize the data entry problems through automated edits, thorough audit trails, and index coding. Automated edits seek to catch errors before they are accepted by the system. They check for accuracy of batch control totals, data sufficiency and format, and a variety of typical mistakes. Edits can also exercise financial controls, such as the rejection of obligations for which unencumbered balances are not available, or vouchers for which approved purchase orders or contracts have not been entered.

Exhaustive audit trails are essential to protect the integrity of any computerized system. They require that significant entries remain logged so it is impossible to erase mistakes without appropriate authorization. Good systems also provide for responsive data editing and verification reports.

Data problems can further be limited by indexing to reduce the characters needed to describe each transaction. Classification with separate digits for each attribute may require in excess of twenty digits, making it difficult to enter transactions with perfect accuracy. However, most transactions can be uniquely identified with fewer than twenty digits through the use of an index code of, say, five or six digits. This reduces workload and errors, while at the same time permitting reports to be written with the designations that have meaning for managers.

EXHIBIT 8–1

FILES MAINTAINED IN TYPICAL INTEGRATED SYSTEMS

- *Transaction History* (holding each transaction for audit and reconciliation purposes)

- *Document Control* (for purchase orders and accounts payable and receivable)

- *Cash Balance*

- *Appropriation Control*

- *Management Reporting* (programs, cost centers, projects)

EXHIBIT 8–2

ACCOUNTING DATA ELEMENTS AND RELATED LEDGER FILES

APPLICABLE LEDGER FILES

Ledger Data Element	Field Size	Budget	Allotment	Plan	Current Detail General Ledger	Summary General Ledger	Current Detail Collection Memo	Summary Collection Memo	Encumbrance Open Items	Vouchers Payable Open Items	Revenue Accrual Open Items	Invoice Open Items
Batch Number	6	x	x	x	x		x		x	x	x	x
Batch Date	6	x	x	x	x		x		x	x	x	x
Transaction Code and Document Number	13	x	x	x	x		x		x	x	x	x
Transaction Date of Record	6	x	x	x	x		x		x	x	x	x
System Acceptance Date	6	x	x	x	x		x		x	x	x	x
Budget Fiscal Year	2	x	x	x	x	x	x	x	x	x	x	x
Accounting Period	5	x	x	x	x	x	x	x	x	x	x	x
Allotment Period	5		x		x	x	x	x	x	x	x	x
Planning Period	5			x	x	x	x	x	x	x	x	x
Document Action (original entry or modification)	1	x	x	x	x		x		x	x	x	x
Line Action (increase or decrease)	1	x	x	x	x		x		x	x	x	x
Type of Purchase Order/Type of Voucher	1				x				x	x		
Vendor Code/Provider Code	8				x		x		x	x	x	x
Vendor Name/Provider Name	30				x		x		x	x	x	x
Document Description	12				x				x	x		
Line Description	30	x			x		x		x	x		
Account Type	2	x	x	x	x	x	x	x	x	x	x	x
Fund	3	x	x	x	x	x	x	x	x	x	x	x
Agency	3	x	x	x	x	x	x	x			x	x
Organization	4	x		x	x	x	x	x				
Sub-Organization	2				x	x	x	x				
Activity	4	x		x	x	x	x	x				
Object of Expenditure	4	x		x	x	x						
Sub-Object	2				x	x						
Revenue Source	4	x		x	x	x	x				x	x
Sub-Revenue Source	2				x	x	x	x				
Balance Sheet Account	4	x			x	x			x	x	x	x
Reporting Category	4				x	x	x	x				
Intra-Government Reference Fund	3	x		x	x	x	x	x	x	x		
Intra-Government Reference Agency	3	x		x	x	x	x	x				
Appropriation Unit	3	x	x	x	x	x						
Bank Account Code	2				x	x	x	x				
Reference Transaction Code and Document Number	13				x		x		x	x	x	x
Debit/Credit Code	1	x	x	x	x	x	x	x	x	x	x	x
Dollar Amount	6	x	x	x	x	x	x	x	x	x	x	x
Open Items Match Key and Status Code	27								x	x	x	x

SOURCE: American Management Systems, Inc.

Flexibility for Modification and Analysis

As needs change, the data base should change. Local governments frequently change their organization, projects of interest, appropriation codes, funding sources, and almost all classifications of data. Further, when an entity such as a responsibility center is changed, this must be reflected in every processing action that utilizes such information; thus the posting logic for appropriations and for all other transactions must be modified to reflect the new responsibility centers. These subsidiary changes can be numerous.

Flexible systems seek to handle such problems in several ways. First, definitions within each dimension or classification are not "hard coded" into the computer posting routines, but, instead, are entered into tables which are looked up automatically each time a transaction is processed. In this way a change in a responsibility center, for example, need only result in a change in the table for responsibility centers, and not in each of the numerous processing steps. Such systems are called "table-driven" systems. Tables are normally used for classification such as account codes, fund codes, program codes, responsibility codes, project codes, and appropriation codes.

Flexibility can also be increased by the use of data base systems. Data base is a method for maintaining the organization of data in computer systems. Where early systems utilized applications programs that specified the detailed location and structure of the data, the data base method allows these concerns to be handled by independent software. When the data base must be changed (for example, by adding a new set of fields in payroll records), the programs that utilize the original data do not have to be modified.

As flexibility in the data base is important, so is flexibility for analysis, especially for the unpredictable and *ad hoc* analysis needed in planning. Modern computer systems facilitate analysis with report and inquiry languages, statistical and modeling packages, and word processing. These innovations made data more accessible to those without programming skills. Inquiry systems and report-writer programs allow untrained staff to write reports with virtually any combination of data, whether or not the system was programmed to produce such a report. This permits quick answers to questions such as, Who are the top users of overtime? or What portion of our contracting goes to in-city vendors?

Statistical and modeling tools (and graphics packages) give significance to patterns of data and are useful for projections. Word processing and text formatting assist in the drafting and redrafting of reports.

Levels of Integration

Financial management information systems can be designed at varying levels of integration. Integration expands the functions handled by a single data base. This tends to improve timeliness and analytic capabilities but, at the same time, also requires a more costly design and operation.

In most applications today, financial functions are handled by *independent systems*—such as payroll, accounting, budgeting, and purchasing—each with its own data entry and processing routines. With independent systems, the data from one function are not used as automated input to another. Thus payroll expenditures are not taken from the payroll system and automatically posted to the general ledger but are handled as a separate and manual accounting task.

The first step toward integration is often to tie together the basic accounting and budgeting functions. This makes certain that budgeting and accounting can use each other's data, and identifies cost and responsibility centers for management control. It should be emphasized that a unified classification system can be designed and implemented while keeping the data processing for each function independent. However, in systems that fully exploit the technology, data collection, and processing are also integrated. Such systems effectively automate much of the work of financial and management reporting.

Medium levels of integration typically reach to the payroll system, and also to the data files on entities involved in financial transactions, such as the personnel files, vendor files, and tax files. Such systems extend their reach far beyond the budget and accounting departments.

In systems with advanced integration, automated modeling and projection tools are also often provided, especially for real estate assessments, budget projections, and investment and portfolio analysis and control. In advanced systems, performance management data can also be kept within the integrated data base. It should be noted, however, that performance data are extremely heterogeneous and typically require separate measures for workload, output, quality, effectiveness, and milestones, each with definitions which change completely from one department to the next. Performance data are rarely collected as a by-product of financial recordkeeping and, in fact, usually require that special new procedures be established. As a result, performance information systems are often independent of the financial information system, but use the same organizational and program structures.

The above descriptions of components of integrated systems are valid in general terms, but details vary. Integration can be applied to selective departments (such as the financial functions of a hospital department—a "vertical" application) or to selective financial functions on a government-wide basis (a "horizontal" application). Exhibit 8–3 suggests progressive levels of integration, and exhibit 8–4 lists some of the typical functions involved.

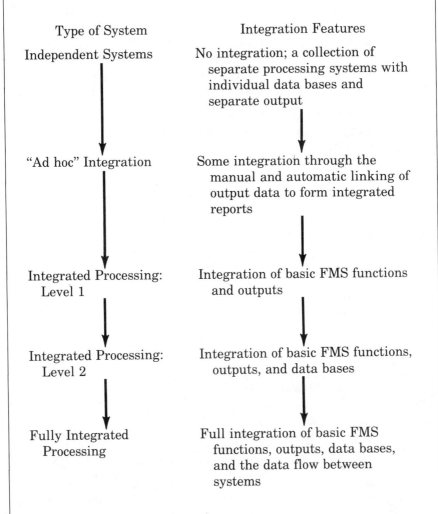

EXHIBIT 8–3

FINANCIAL MANAGEMENT SYSTEMS:
PROGRESSIVE LEVELS OF INTEGRATION

Type of System	Integration Features
Independent Systems	No integration; a collection of separate processing systems with individual data bases and separate output
"Ad hoc" Integration	Some integration through the manual and automatic linking of output data to form integrated reports
Integrated Processing: Level 1	Integration of basic FMS functions and outputs
Integrated Processing: Level 2	Integration of basic FMS functions, outputs, and data bases
Fully Integrated Processing	Full integration of basic FMS functions, outputs, data bases, and the data flow between systems

SOURCE: Kenneth L. Kraemer and John Leslie King. "Financial Management Systems: Independent and Integrated Design." In *Computers in Local Government: Finance and Administration*. Prepared by the editorial staff of Auerbach Publishers in consultation with Kenneth L. Kraemer and John Leslie King. 1980.

EXHIBIT 8–4

FUNCTIONS INCLUDED IN INTEGRATED FINANCIAL
INFORMATION SYSTEMS

Basic Accounting Functions and Reporting

• Transaction registers
• Outstanding encumbrances and invoices
• Appropriations status
• Spending and revenues against budgets for cost centers, projects, and programs
• Cash balances
• Trial balances for balance sheets and operating statements

Secondary and Specialized Functions

• Payroll accounting and preparation
• Purchasing, including vendor files with P.O. preparation
• Billing and accounts receivable
• Fixed asset and inventory control
• Work order and job cost control

Advanced Financial Management Functions

• Performance measurement
• Real estate assessment
• Position control
• Budget preparation and projection aids

SOURCE: Adapted from C. Wayne Stallings. "Integrated Financial Management Systems: Key Features and Implementation Considerations." In *Computers in Local Government: Finance and Administration.* Prepared by the editorial staff of Auerbach Publishers, Inc. with consultation of Kenneth L. Kraemer and John Leslie King. 1980.

Benefits and Costs of Integrated Systems

Integrated systems are a working reality in an increasing number of localities. No government, however, should choose a new system casually, since the consequences are major. Both benefits and costs should be closely examined.

The Purposes and Benefits of Integrated Systems

Local governments are funded and regulated by the financial market and by local, state, and federal agencies. The financial relationships are increasingly complex. In sorting through complex data and helping with required reports, good information systems can both make money and save money; they can do this by strengthening relationships with external agencies, and by improving the process of internal planning and control.

Financial Reporting and Disclosure. A capacity to aggregate transaction data in a form meeting generally accepted accounting principles is a key feature of the modern integrated computerized system. Because expenditures and revenues are recorded at each of a series of discrete stages including (in the case of expenditures) encumbrance or obligation, receipt of goods or services, billing and disbursement, much of the data needed for accrual accounting are readily available.

Well-designed computer systems can reduce the costs of preparing comprehensive annual financial reports, including the costs of external auditing. Further, the computer can help with interim reporting, the preparation of official disclosure statements for investors, and the variety of summaries needed by internal managers, political leaders, and the general public.

Grants Reporting. The integrated information system also makes it possible to automate reporting on grant-financed projects. In the last fifteen years, federal aid to state and local governments increased sevenfold, and by 1979 there were eighty different audit guides by fourteen federal agencies. The growth in grant-related reporting has been enormous: Medicaid, CETA, CDBG, Affirmative Action, UDAGs, just to mention a few. Grants reporting requires much of the same data as other financial reporting, but often calls for different time periods, a different accounting basis, or specialized funding sources. There is an increasing tendency for federal agencies to move towards a single-audit approach, and to require reporting on a modified accrual basis; indeed, such a requirement may be imposed on all federal grants in the foreseeable future.

Reimbursement-eligible expenditures together with allocated indirect costs and allowances for the use of depreciable facilities and equipment can be cumulated automatically on advanced systems for each grant-supported project or activity. This helps assure both full cost reimbursement and prompt billing.

Cost Accounting.   Cost accounting for specified projects and activities can, similarly, be programmed into the information system and related to output and performance data. This requires special provision only where depreciation data are desired for activities or projects financed through governmental funds.

Planning and Analysis.   Integrated systems usually produce better data than independent systems and also provide more powerful tools for its manipulation. Studies easily accomplished with integrated systems can be so difficult with other systems that they are rarely even attempted. Examples include the cost accounting mentioned above and "what if" budget projections based on a variety of labor settlement and inflation possibilities.

In general, automated systems can present an overview of the forest before breaking it down to individual trees. *This capacity to move back and forth from summary to detail is absent in many existing systems and is key to helping managers and analysts develop a clear understanding and "feel" for their data.*

Control.   Control is enhanced under an integrated and automated system. This is because it is possible to monitor both expenditures and performance more closely with the more timely and more detailed information available. Cost-center managers can be measured against agreed-on performance targets. The system records the targets and supplies feedback needed for variance meetings to decide on corrective actions that may be needed. While information alone will not insure that management is effectively controlled, the ability to control without it is extremely limited.

Receivables Management.   Prompter billing and collection of taxes, grants, and other receivables should be realized. In addition, better management of accounts payable is likely.

Cash Management.   Savings in short-term interest costs (or increased earnings on short-term investments) are greatly facilitated by an automated financial information system.

The Costs and Risks of Integrated Systems

By their very nature, integrated systems require a somewhat revolutionary abandonment of preexisting systems. There are obviously costs and risks to any such endeavor.

Low Ongoing Costs. While data entry is complicated with integrated systems, the major ongoing costs are for the management time and analytic talent needed to exploit improved information. There are also risks in dependency on a sophisticated computer that can go down completely when a single subsystem goes down. All things considered, however, the incremental ongoing costs of integrated systems are not high, and are outweighed by cost savings and improved revenues.

Significant Implementation Costs and Risks. The major problems with integrated systems involve implementation. While these can be smoothed by careful planning and organization, they are by no means trivial. Effective implementation requires a rare combination of technical and organizational expertise. Talented staff must typically be assigned on a full-time basis for a year or more, with specialized consulting support also required. Standard steps in the process are illustrated in exhibit 8–5.

Local governments that have implemented integrated systems have, typically, overrun budgeted costs and time frame by a factor of two to five. Even with successful systems, problems have tended to follow yet other problems before the new systems could be made to work right.

However severe the technical complexities, the major problems are usually those of bureaucratic and political turbulence. Information systems are designed for clarity and accountability. However, as almost everyone knows intuitively, there are times when clarity looks dangerous and confusion seems a comfort. Many local governments have a tradition of fragmentation, partly as a check against the accumulation of too much power, and partly for access and responsiveness to the public. New information systems may threaten existing power relationships.

Benefits vs. Costs

In balancing benefits against costs, the choice is complicated by options that include a wide variety of improvements in functional systems as an alternative to fully integrated systems. The pros and cons of independent versus integrated systems are reviewed and summarized in exhibit 8–6.

In general, it seems clear that integrated systems are complicated and risky to implement. If handled successfully, however, they provide substantial net benefits through improved reporting, more efficient data collection and processing, and better capacity for analysis. While few benefit-cost studies have documented the case for highly integrated systems, one study for the city of Dayton suggests that a $2.9 million investment generated a savings of $658,000 per year (see exhibit 8–7).

The economic case for computerized, integrated financial information systems in local government has become progressively stronger. There is

EXHIBIT 8–5

STEPS IN THE SYSTEMS DEVELOPMENT PROCESS

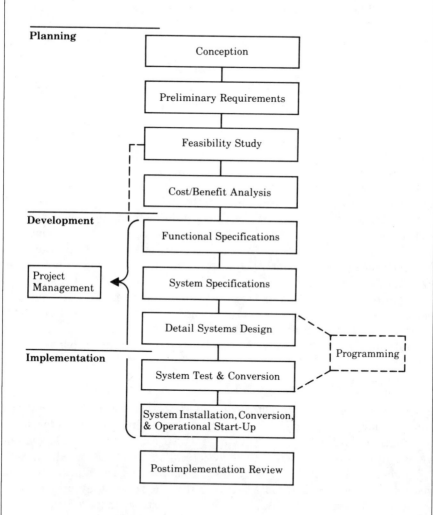

SOURCE: Dr. Ralph Young. "Managing the Systems Development Process." In *Computers in Local Government: Finance and Administration*. Prepared by the editorial staff of Auerbach Publishers in consultation with Kenneth L. Kraemer and John Leslie King. 1980.

EXHIBIT 8–6

PROS AND CONS OF INDEPENDENT AND INTEGRATED FINANCIAL
MANAGEMENT SYSTEMS

	PROS	**CONS**
Independent FMS	1. Generally less expensive to build	1. Computing capability of system is not fully utilized
	2. Modular in structure	2. Nonstandard uses of the system are limited
	3. Manageable as units	3. Integrating data from several sources may be difficult
	4. Many operational systems that conform to current financial procedures	4. Systems and data must be linked manually
	5. Systems can be discarded or modified without damaging other systems	5. Different coding schemes used by different systems make linkages difficult
	6. Failure of one system does not bring down others	6. Input and output data are decentralized making access costly and inconsistencies and errors more likely
	7. Relatively low level of data processing sophistication required	7. Meeting management and planning requests is constrained by design limitations

continued

Integrated FMS	1. Greater exploitation of computing potential	1. Generally more expensive and complex to build
	2. Complex and nonstandard analyses can be routinely accommodated	2. System must be planned and designed as a cohesive unit
	3. System can be used to organize and integrate standard operations	3. System requires advanced and sophisticated technology to build and maintain
	4. Data are standardized and centralized increasing consistency of information and improving access	4. Start-up often plagued by hard-to-solve problems
	5. Manual transcription for linking data is eliminated	5. Failure of one subsystem may cause the failure of the entire system
	6. Consistent input formats and coding schemes allow for easier internal changes	6. System may cause organizational disruption
	7. New outputs based on the existing data base are accommodated as easily as standard outputs	7. Possible error propagation in data

SOURCE: Kenneth L. Kraemer and John Leslie King. "Financial Management Systems: Independent and Integrated Design." In *Computers in Local Government: Finance and Administration*. Prepared by the editorial staff of Auerbach Publishers in consultation with Kenneth L. Kraemer and John Leslie King. 1980.

EXHIBIT 8–7

FINANCIAL INFORMATION SYSTEMS: SAVINGS VS. COSTS
DAYTON, OHIO

Annual Savings:

Improved cash management (investment income)	$300,000
Budget preparation (cost displacement)	250,000
Reports and projections for budget review (value)	100,000
Equipment savings from EDP consolidation	8,000
Total, annual savings	$658,000

One-Time Savings:

Not replacing bookkeeping machines	$ 90,000

Cost of System (federally financed costs) $2.9 million

SOURCE: City of Dayton, *Public Finance Municipal Information Subsystem, Final Project Report.* No. H-1212 (PFS) - 1. National Technical Information Service. Springfield, Virginia. 1975. Cited in Kenneth L. Kraemer and John Leslie King. *Integrated Financial Management Systems: Dayton Case Study.* 1980.

little doubt that the trend will continue. This reflects three different factors. First, there is, for most local governments, no other efficient means of satisfying the standards for financial management and reporting demanded by grantors and lenders. Second, technological advances in computer hardware are continuing to both reduce the cost of data management and to extend automation to smaller and smaller units. Third, there is now an abundance of both appropriate software already tested in pioneer applications and technical support in computer, consulting, and service firms.

Strategic and Implementation Considerations

Whatever the benefits, strategic choices are required in the selection and implementation of new financial systems. To avoid the major dangers—getting bogged down in the bureaucratic swamp or stuck in the technical brambles—the following six points are relevant.

Picking the Entry Point

Some governments have a strong tradition of management or a political leadership committed to management improvement. In such a case, the only requirement for starting a new information system may be a clear policy decision.

Often, however, there may be conflicting issues, or a history of prior failures of efforts at management improvement. Here it is wise to start with a project, however simple, where the balance of power is clearly supportive. The entry project should be consistent with a longer-term integrated system, and should be used to help build the expertise and support needed for the longer-term effort.

A variety of projects present "first-step" possibilities. They tend to be vertical systems, or those within the jurisdiction of a strong and supportive manager. Good entry points may also be projects "required" by external agencies or constituencies. It is important to keep in mind the fact that going too fast could risk future programs as well as the immediate project.

Picking the Approach

Once an entry point is selected, success requires an effective technical and organizational approach. If technical problems are the prime concern, prepackaged software can often reduce the likelihood of technical failures. Technical problems can also be reduced through use of an outside service bureau or facility manager to operate the system. In either case, however, some loss in responsiveness to unique local problems is likely.

If, on the other hand, the primary concern is to avoid organizational disruption, systems can be custom designed to closely mimic current procedures. This generally makes for easier training and acceptance, but requires more computer and accounting expertise. It should be mentioned that some packaged applications also have latitude for substantial special-tailoring, and several of the new extremely high-level programming languages can also reduce the technical problems of custom-designed applications.

In either case—whether going for a packaged application or a specially tailored design—an age-old approach is to go for demonstrated success. Apparently successful applications at other sites should be sought out and carefully reviewed before trying to transfer them. Site visits may be desirable especially to help assess the quality of implementation support provided by the vendor.

Maintaining Top-Level Involvement

Strategies to destabilize an equilibrium and reestablish it in a more favorable position require cooperation or at least the tolerance of other critical actors. This is one of the strongest arguments for starter projects promising short-term success.

If the top-level support is upfront and visible, it may isolate the potential opposition and make it easier to develop momentum. However, in using the symbols of power to get a project started, it is safest if the initial commitment includes the funding and staff needed for the entire project. In this way, retracting the commitment requires action rather than inaction. Systems projects tend to take a long time and require a lot of attention to detail.

Allowing Time and Resources for Training

It is hard to overestimate the importance of training, yet it is often handled poorly. To implement a new system well, representatives of affected groups should be involved in development. Both classroom and on-the-job training should be provided. Education and training should rapidly merge into full-time operation, lest new skills be lost. Training should work first with groups likely to be supportive, with the best participants helping to train others.

It is important throughout for the local project team to have access to technical expertise independent of the vendors, even if this expertise must also be provided by consultants. Another point to remember is that consultants who are good at technical systems design are often not so good at training and support.

Developing an Integrated Design

No matter what the entry project, an early conceptual study of the overall system is essential. While much can be done with relatively independent vertical systems, no major change in a horizontal system should be undertaken without first seeing that linkages to other components have been allowed for or already designed. Building a sophisticated computer system is somewhat like constructing a building. It can be very hard to make small changes not anticipated in the original plan.

Modular design and implementation is often appropriate. Modules can fit together, yet be implemented individually without overwhelming the capacities of the bureaucracy. Talent can thus be focused rather than spread too thin. In any case, the conceptual design of the final goal should come early; it should develop the functional requirements and basis for guiding the remainder of the development process.

Adding Long-Term Elements

As important as it is to pick a good entry point, it is equally important to add long-term elements so the early momentum will not be lost. A broad but sometimes overlooked tactic is to be certain that follow-up projects are underway before existing projects are completed.

For example, the city of Boston began a financial management improvement project of an independent audit which was needed to preserve the city's access to the bond market. The strategy called for a *three-year audit management program* and for loading the auditors with an extensive agenda of management analysis. Before the first financial statements and management letter had been completed, the city had spun off several "vertical" projects to develop new financial information systems:

- Completely new accounting, budgeting, and payroll systems for the health and hospitals department
- A packaged software, minicomputer system (funded by the federal government) for a stand-alone CETA agency
- A custom-designed governmentwide personnel and performance measurement system developed on another minicomputer in the Office of Management and Budget

By means of these projects, Boston made substantial progress and developed some in-house computer and project skill needed for the larger horizontal projects that remain for the future.

Summing Up: Integrated Information Systems

Over the next five years, local governments—large and small—will face key decisions about computerized and integrated financial management information systems. The demands for improved reporting and management will grow, as will the availability of cheaper and more sophisticated computer technologies. While inaction will exact high opportunity costs, so will short-sighted action that fails to allow for long-term needs. Political leaders and managers alike should be aware of the issues and ready to attack targets of opportunity. While caution and incrementalism are warranted, strategic steps can begin now toward the goal of more useful and integrated systems.

The computerized financial information system offers major opportunities to better link financial management functions through an integrated data base. In larger local governments, such a system is essential to integrated financial management. In nearly all local governments, regardless of size, it will be the most effective and efficient approach to the collection, management, and reporting of financial and performance data.

Auditing and Program Evaluation 9

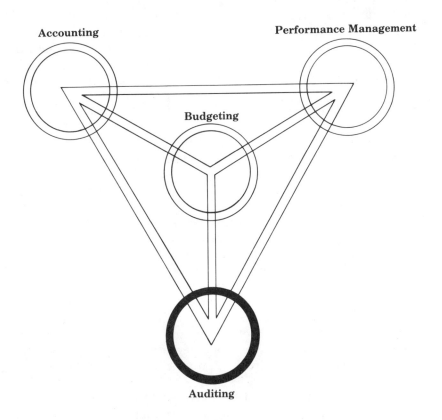

Accounting

Performance Management

Budgeting

Auditing

"the feedback loop"

The financial management system, as it has been discussed in the preceding chapters, includes all of the elements basic to its internal functioning. The well-developed financial management system provides for its legislators, its chief executive, and its citizens an abundance of information from which the quality of performance and financial condition can be assessed. In addition, procedures for financial and performance accountability and for budget review and analysis provide some assurance the salient issues will be identified and addressed.

What accounting, budgeting, and performance management do not provide is an independent assessment of the operations and reports of local government. Such an assessment is needed not only by the purchasers, underwriters, and raters or the locality's notes and bonds, the federal and state grant-making agencies and members of the legislative body but, also, by the chief executive and the principal officials of the executive branch.

Independent assessment involves three different issues:

- The integrity of the functioning of the financial management system—whether the financial reports fairly reflect the financial position of the locality under generally accepted accounting principles, whether the safeguards against unauthorized expenditure are adequate, whether required procedures are consistently followed, and whether cost and performance are accurately reported.
- *The quality of management*—the extent to which program performance meets achievable standards of quality and efficiency.
- *The effectiveness of programs*—whether, for example, an increase in police manpower had any impact upon the crime rate or the apprehension of criminals; whether a new training program resulted in a significant number of job placements or if the trainees were retained in such jobs; whether school performance of underpriviledged children was improved by a remedial education program; or whether cleaner streets resulted from a new street cleaning program.

These are questions that can be answered only by an after-the-fact review and evaluation performed by organizations and individuals independent of those responsible for the activities that are evaluated. The audit is the established form for such an evaluation.

The independent audit has been associated primarily with financial and compliance matters, but it may embrace *any* of the issues cited. Issues involving program performance and results may, alternatively, be assessed through program evaluation studies carried out by organizations or individuals without the accounting credentials of auditors.

It is easy to understand why those outside the executive branch need an independent assessment of the information reported and the representations made by executive officials. It may not be equally obvious why independent audits and evaluations are important to the chief executives and their chief aides. The basic reason is that the chief executive, even in a well managed local government, can ordinarily be no more certain than outsiders about the accuracy and completeness of reporting and the effectiveness of financial controls. The executive may be—but more often is not—better informed about how the efficiency and quality of local program performance compare to standards achieved elsewhere but will, typically, have little hard information in program outcomes.

Audits and evaluations constitute the feedback loop in the financial system. They provide the periodic check-ups necessary to assure that the machinery of the system is functioning satisfactorily and to identify areas for correction. They can add second opinions on the quality of managment that often prove valuable and supply information not otherwise available on actual program outcomes.

The Types of Audit

An audit, in the sense in which we use the term, is always an independent *ex post* review. Under this definition, the so-called "pre-audit," which is common in municipal government, is not an audit at all but, rather, a review of transactions prior to final approval that should properly be regarded as an aspect of the accounting and budget control processes.

The United States General Accounting Office describes the audit function as embracing three different elements or types of audit:

> *Financial and compliance audits*—to determine (a) whether financial operations are properly conducted, (b) whether the financial reports of an audited entity are presented fairly, and (c) whether the entity has complied with applicable laws and regulations.   •
> *Economy and efficiency audits*—to determine whether the entity is managing or utilizing its resources (personnel, property, space, and so forth) in an economical and efficient manner and the causes of any inefficiencies or uneconomical practices, including inadequacies in management information systems, administrative procedures, or organizational structures.
> *Program results audits*—to determine whether the desired results or benefits are being achieved, whether the objectives established by the legislature or other authorizing body are being met, and whether the agency has considered alternatives which might yield desired results at a lower cost.

The first of these, the financial and compliance audit, is the basic, established form of audit essential to any assessment of the financial reports of local government. Audits of economy and efficiency and of program results, while not uncommon, are performed in a relatively small proportion of local governments. The three different audit elements may either all be included in a comprehensive audit or performed separately.

The Financial and Compliance Audit

The objectives of the financial and compliance audit are

- The expression of an opinion that the financial statements of the local government present its financial position and results of operations in conformity with generally accepted accounting principles
- To ascertain whether, in obtaining and expending public funds, the locality has complied with the applicable statutes

The generally accepted auditing standards (or GAAS) of the American Institute of Certified Public Accountants provide the authoritative guidelines for the conduct of financial audits of both private organizations and governments. The United States General Accounting Office has incorporated them in its publication, *Standards for Audit of Governmental Organizations, Programs, Activities and Functions.*

The auditors must be independent of the audited organization. They can have no direct or indirect interest in the financial affairs of either that organization or its officers. A government auditor is not regarded as independent if he or she is responsible for maintaining the accounts being audited or reports to the person with that responsibility. The auditor may be elected or appointed but cannot report to the chief executive or to any official of the executive branch of the audited local government. Many government audit staffs do not meet this standard of independence. They may perform highly professional and useful audits and evaluations but for an independent financial and compliance audit, the local government must rely on licensed or certified public accountants in private practice or, in some cases, on state auditors.

The audit report must, under GAAS, include an opinion on the financial statements, a comparison of accounting principles actually followed by the audited organization with generally accepted accounting principles, and information on all facts material to the financial reports or compliance with legal requirements. The work performed under the audit must include a study of the government's system of internal control sufficient to determine the reliability of accounting data and the collection of evidence adequate to support an opinion as to whether the financial statements fairly represent the financial condition of the local government.

These are minimum requirements. The audited local government can negotiate with its auditors for a more extensive or more detailed work program. For example, the review of the internal control system need be no more extensive than is necessary to determine the reliability of accounting data; an expanded effort would ordinarily be necessary for a full evaluation of the effectiveness of the internal control system.

The Economy and Efficiency Audit

The economy and efficiency audit is more commonly known as a management or operational or performance audit. It bears a close resemblance to some management studies. An audit of this character is concerned with the quality of management structure and organization as well as the operational performance. It identifies the extent and apparent causes of inefficiencies, failures to achieve management objectives, and deviations from managerial policies. Recommendations are made for corrective action.

The periodic appraisal of the performance of local government agencies is highly desirable. Economy and efficiency audits are not inexpensive but should not be necessary more often than once every three to five years for most agencies. An audit program might include a schedule designed to cover all agencies and programs over a five-year cycle.

The appraisal of performance can but need not be done as an independent audit. The approach makes sense for a local legislative body interested in a wholly independent review of executive performance. For the same reasons, it is a logical extension of the work of state and local audit agencies.

On the other hand, the chief executive and his department heads will often prefer a management study under executive control. Yet, the independent audit of performance can offer significant advantages to executive management. In programs where significant improvement in performance is indicated, the independence of the audit approach adds to the credibility of its findings; this may be important where there is resistance to change among agency managers or in employee unions, or reluctance in the legislative body to commit the funds required for management improvement. In agencies where efficiency is high, the audit can provide verification in a public forum that this is, in fact, so.

The Program Results Audit

The program results audit is, for all practical purposes, a form of program evaluation. Program evaluations, like other audits, are usually conducted under circumstances designed to assure their independence of executive management.

The extent to which programs and operations achieve their intended results is often not apparent even to those responsible for the management of those programs. Frequently, programs are conceived, justified, and operated under assumptions that are never verified.

A rigorous program evaluation format may require elaborate measures, such as the tracking of program participants for long periods after program completion and the establishment of control groups as a means of determining what might have occurred in the absence of the program. This is difficult under the format and timing of the typical program results audit unless data have been collected under an evaluation plan from the inception of the program. If an extensive program evaluation study is needed, it is probably usually best done outside the audit structure by an organization with special competence in evaluation techniques or in the particular subject matter. This depends, of course, on the skills available in the audit organization.

Less ambitious evaluations will usually be adequate to meet local objectives. Program results audits and evaluations tend to be more useful in some program areas than in others. Examples of program areas in which evaluation may be especially worthwhile include the following:

- Manpower training and vocational education (What proportions of participants complete the program and are placed in training-relevant jobs?)
- Remedial education (What is the impact upon achievement scores?)
- Criminal investigation (What proportion of crimes of what kind are solved through criminal investigation?)
- Sanitation (How is street cleanliness related to street sweeping and refuse collection?)
- Code enforcement (To what extent does it result in corrective action?)

For new programs of this character, it makes sense to provide for the design of the evaluation at the time the program is authorized.

Program audits and evaluations can produce information of extraordinary usefulness to local decision makers. Programs with very reasonable costs per unit workload often prove to have astronomical costs per unit of results actually achieved. Audit findings should provide a basis for terminating some marginal programs and for changing others. Most important, however, is the fact that keeping score in problem-solving orientation in program managers that can lead to better performance.

Other Types of Audits

Two other types of audit are worthy of note.

The Internal Audit. An internal audit process can be conducted within the executive branch either on a governmentwide basis, or, more often, separately for each major department. An internal audit does not meet the standards for an independent audit because it is conducted under the overall direction of an official reporting to an operating executive. However, a well-managed internal audit process can, in fact, be run with nearly as much independence as an outside independent audit. To assure this degree of independence, the internal audit unit should be independent of accounting and budgeting with its director reporting to the chief executive of the department or agency. Internal audit may sometimes, however, be one element of a broader unit concerned with inspection of functions with a high potential for criminal offenses and the investigation of allegation of criminal behavior.

The internal audit, unlike the independent financial compliance audit, does not result in an auditor's opinion of the financial statements of the local government. With this exception, it may cover any or all of the subjects included in the three types of independent audit.

The purpose of internal audit is to aid management. It will ordinarily include elements of both financial and management audits. The internal audit has the advantage to program and departmental executives of being able to uncover and correct major problems in accountability and management prior to their exposure in an independent external audit. At the same time, it greatly increases the productivity and effectiveness of the external auditors since they can use the worksheets and notes of the internal auditors as a starting point for their own work. Indeed, it is probably fair to say that external auditing of a complex government is unlikely to be fully effective until there is also a well-developed and professional internal audit function.

Performance System Audit. Audits of performance measurement systems are beginning to be seen by public officials as a useful approach to testing validity of the system's results and to building credibility for their productivity efforts. In some cases, organizations outside government, such as business advisory councils or citizen fiscal research agencies, are called upon to audit or evaluate performance measurement systems.

Planning and Managing an Audit Program

In most local governments, the audit process has been governed by legal requirements, professional standards, and the needs of lenders, underwriters and grantors. We believe that a local government should go beyond these externally determined requirements and develop a program of audits and evaluations that meets its own managerial needs. To start your thinking about the audit process, we recommend that you read *Local Government Auditing: A Manual for Public Officials*, a concise explanation of auditing published by the Council on Municipal Performance (COMP) with assistance from the Department of Housing and Urban Development. (The complete citation is in the Bibliography.)

The Council on Municipal Performance suggests assigning local responsibility for planning and managing audits to an audit committee including legislators and, possibly, private citizens as well as financial management officials. This makes a lot of sense and provides the potential for a broader perspective of the audit process.

A multiyear plan is especially desirable for management and program audits or evaluations. Decisions should be made on those agencies and programs where an independent review of managerial performance and/or program results appears to be most needed. A plan might, for example, call for an audit of one high priority area each year. With the agencies or programs identified in advance, it is possible to develop a detailed statement of coverage concentrating on the aspects of greatest local importance.

The same approach can be taken toward supplemental aspects of the financial audit. Local officials may decide that certain areas require more detailed attention than they can be given in the standard financial and compliance audit. Purchasing and procurement procedures, user charge pricing, cash collections, and the processing and payment of vendor bills are illustrative subject areas. A plan might call for expanding the annual audit to include one or two of these special problem areas each year. The choices might be based upon the incidence of known problems or upon the relative importance or sensitivity of the operation involved. In some cases, the work may involve elements of a management audit.

A broad program of audits and evaluations should include both independent audits and internal audits. A local government may, for example, rely on an internal audit staff for all but the basic independent financial and compliance audit. This depends upon the extent the particular area needs study from a wholly independent perspective and upon the skills available in the internal staff. Similarly, the locality can select from a wide variety of outside specialists for aspects of the program other than the financial and compliance audit.

The COMP publication previously cited provides excellent guidance on planning and managing the annual financial and compliance audit. It is especially important to establish clearly the scope of the work to be performed and the issues to be addressed in the auditor's management letter which, simply because it addresses management issues, is usually more useful to local officials than the audit report itself. The local government should provide for some organized approach to the auditor's findings and recommendations. An audit committee of the kind previously suggested provides a good forum for doing this.

Those local governments where audits are performed by an official of the state or local government may have less flexibility in determining the scope and character of audits than those localities engaging auditors and evaluators from the private sector. However, in the federal government and in many states and cities, much of the work of the auditing office is done at the instruction or request of the legislative body or its committees. There is, further, no reason why the chief executive cannot request the state or local government to address areas of special concern. In addition, it is usually possible to engage outside accountants and evaluators to conduct studies the government auditor cannot undertake.

Summing Up: Audits and Other Fiscal Systems

The audit, because of the need for assuring its independence, tends not to be regarded as an integral element of the financial management system. Yet, it provides the evaluation crucial to the effective functioning of other parts of the system.

A local program of audits and evaluations should provide for economy and efficiency audits and programs results audits as well as financial and compliance audits. It should include both internal and independent audits.

An annual financial and compliance audit conducted according to generally accepted auditing standards is essential. The financial audit should be extended to provide more extensive examination of areas of special concern to the executive or the legislative body. In addition, there should be a regular program for the auditing of management performance and program results in agencies and programs involving issues or questions of high significance to local officials.

The independent financial and compliance audit not only serves those who lend or grant funds to the local government but also provides local officials with a needed annual check-up on their management and reporting of financial transactions. Management (or economy and efficiency) audits are a means of obtaining a valuable second opinion on performance in key agencies. Program audits and evaluations help determine whether certain programs are worth their costs.

Chief executives, department heads, and members of the legislative body need audits and evaluations as a means of insuring the integrity of the local management system. They cannot assume, without checking, that financial transactions are properly managed, controlled, and reported. They cannot assume, without investigation, that expected program results are actually being achieved. An integrated budgeting, accounting, and performance management system incorporates procedures for correction and improvement. The addition of audit and evaluation helps make sure they really work.

Strategies for Integration 10

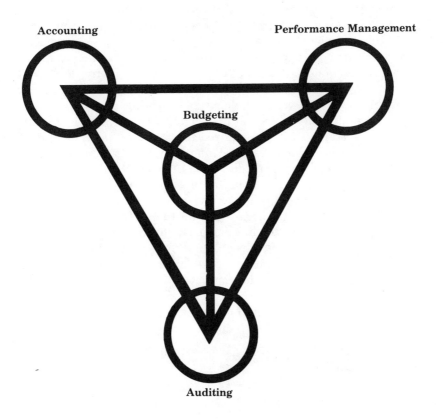

Accounting

Performance Management

Budgeting

Auditing

"starting points for any community"

The place to start, for the officials of any local government considering a program to improve and better interrelate their financial management functions, is by thinking about the problem and developing at least a rough sense of strategy. Let's begin with a few general observations that bear on the development of a strategy:

- Financial management should be developed as the centerpiece of the government's overall management system. It is not an esoteric matter that should be left entirely to technicians.
- A sustained five-to-ten-year effort will typically be required to achieve a fully developed integrated financial management system.
- Getting everyone together on an improvement program is important and, in some local governments, critical. Financial management involves the budget director, the finance director, the auditor, the assessor, the local legislature, the chief executive, and, to a lesser but important extent, officials of the operating agencies.
- Some significant incremental expenditures—especially for information systems—will be required in most local governments. The exceptions are those local governments with financial management functions already well advanced and those small enough to function without large investments in information systems.
- Potential cash benefits—in savings or increased revenues are also likely to be significant. A strategy for the early realization of these benefits may be feasible in some local governments.
- There is no rigidly prescribed series of steps to achieve a fully developed system. What makes sense for any given local government will depend, in part, on the character of its financial management operations at the time the improvement effort is initiated. But even two governments with similar characteristics and situations could, quite rationally, decide on a different sequence of improvements.

These considerations are discussed at somewhat greater detail in the sections that follow.

Organizing for Financial Integration

The Financial Management Improvement Committee

Many years ago, the federal government began a continuing effort to improve the quality of financial management. Because three different agencies were heavily involved in financial management, the effort was conducted as a Joint Financial Management Improvement Program (initially, the Joint Accounting Improvement Program) in which the Bureau of the Budget (now the Office of Management and Budget), the Department of the Treasury, and the General Accounting Office all participated.

There are similar divisions of responsibility in most local governments and, consequently, a similar need to establish an approach involving the different financial management agencies in the policy direction and coordination of the improvement program. A Financial Management Improvement Committee is an excellent device to help meet this need. Such a committee might include the following officials:

- Director of the budget
- Director of finance
- Chief auditor
- Chairman, city, town or county council, finance committee
- Mayor, city or county manager, or county executive

Representation of some operating agencies should also be considered. The committee would develop basic policies and strategies, identify priorities, review proposed projects, and assess progress from time to time. The committee would also provide a degree of continuity that is often absent in individual agencies due to turnover in managerial positions.

The committee need not have managerial responsibilities since most improvement projects will fall within the functions of the separate agencies represented on the committee, or, sometimes, within the scope of the operating agencies. Secretariat duties could be assigned to an official of one of the participating financial management agencies.

The strategy for financial management improvement should be based upon a perception of needs shared by those involved in the management of the locality and its financial management system. In some local governments—especially some of the city manager cities in the West and Southwest—the environment has tended to be conductive to managerial innovation making it relatively easy to reach a consensus that the local government should proceed to the development of an advanced comprehensive financial management system.

In more traditional governments, attitudes about both the desirability and feasibility of major improvements are likely to be more skeptical; in these governments, perceived needs are likely to involve more modest changes and to be directed toward problems on which there is some external pressure for an early solution, say, from state or federal funding agencies or state auditors. Even in governments of this character, however, discussions in a financial management improvement committee are likely to generate a more extensive list of problems and needs. The financial management official seemingly most content with the existing arrangements is likely to concede, if pressed, that "ideally, of course, we would like to have. . . ."

Staffing the Effort

Except in the smallest governments, progress is unlikely if it depends upon the ability of already overcommitted senior staff to find time to work on financial management improvement. At a minimum, a substantial part of the time of an appropriate staff member in budget or accounting or both should be committed to the effort at its initiation to help set out options and costs and to assure interagency communication and follow-up.

More staff will be required as specific projects are undertaken to advance integration. If the budget bureau is to analyze programs and issues, it must have the staff to do it. Consultants may be engaged to develop the information system required but the local government must have a competent staff to develop the specifications and manage the consulting contract. The operating agencies participating will need to hire or reassign staff to carry out their responsibilities under the program.

If resources are limited, staff additions can be held to very small numbers—at the cost, of course, of slower progress. The important point is that a financial management improvement and integration program will require staff and funding.

The Use of Consultants

Comparatively few local governments will be able to do the job without some use of outside consultants and contractors. Much of the work of installing an integrated financial management information system will, in the vast majority of cases, be entrusted to an outside provider. On many other aspects of financial management improvement, consultants will often be necessary or desirable to supplement time and skills available from local staff.

There is no foolproof method for selecting a consultant, but there are a few helpful practices:

- Do not limit consideration to a single firm but, rather, identify three or more firms that have done work of the kind required and solicit proposals from all of them.
- Check out their performance with officials of the governments for which they have done work.
- Meet with principals of the various firms to discuss costs, time period, possible problems, and options.
- Staff training, where appropriate, should be included in the contract.

The local government should assign competent staff to the project with enough time to maintain liaison with the consultants and to monitor and evaluate their work. If there is no available staff person technically competent to do this, consider employing an expert from a nearby university or other source on a per diem basis to assist in supervising the work of the consultant. Such an expert may, in fact, be useful even earlier in developing the specifications for the consultant contract.

Identifying Problems, Needs, Opportunities, and Issues

Rarely will the problems in the performance of the financial management system be fully evident. Usually, however, some of them will have been exposed and pressure created for their solution. Some will be purely financial. For example,

- Failure to meet financial management requirements under federal grant programs
- Deficiencies identified in federal, state, or local audit reports
- Spending in excess or appropriations in some programs or agencies
- Underbudgeting of expenditures and/or overestimation of revenues
- Complaints of delays in issuing vendor payments, payroll checks, or tax refunds
- Excessive tax delinquency

Other financial problems may be exposed only through investigation. For example,

- Excessive noninterest bearing cash balances
- Underbilling for federal and other reimbursement
- Delays between receipt and deposit of funds

Problems of inadequate information on expenditures tend to be common. These are especially important in agencies and programs where the lack of information is coupled with public, legislative, or high level executive complaints on performance.

Shortcomings in the performance of major public programs are also important. Programs that attract large numbers of citizen complaints or where observed performance is patently deficient probably need better managers, but they also, usually, need better systems for managing performance and expenditures.

The opportunities will typically be problems viewed from a different perspective. One general opportunity should not be ignored. Any situation conducive—by virtue if scandal, complaints, reorganization, the appointment of a new administrator or any other factor—to management reform is an opportunity for improving the financial management system in that agency.

One important group of opportunities are those involving operations for which responsibility is vested entirely or predominantly in the financial management agencies. In these cases, there are usually no significant potential employee relations or work force problems, no threatened interests of program clients, and no difficulties in securing the cooperation of the heads of the operating agencies.

A local government may elect to focus its financial management improvement projects on areas where significant budgetary savings are likely. It might, on the other hand, decide to concentrate on activities under criticism by citizens or funding agencies. Another approach is to select areas where the costs of system development will be borne in the main from federal or state funding.

It is also necessary to identify the deficiencies in the existing financial management system, whether or not they are the source of any current problems or opportunities. This can be done by comparing the existing system, item by item, with the elements of an integrated financial management system outlined in the introduction to this guide. Use the checklist in chapter 2, as well, to identify shortcomings.

The inventory of problems and opportunities should be used in setting priorities for action. A plan for financial management improvement is likely to be more realistic and to be more easily justified if it addresses concrete needs.

Developing a Plan

Few local governments will be able to start with a highly detailed plan. A plan should, at minimum, include the following:

- A detailing of the first steps to be taken—say, those to be initiated before the end of the next fiscal year
- An indication of how these first steps relate to those elements of the financial improvement effort to be undertaken in subsequent years
- A comprehensive outline of the overall plan, plus a general notion of how it is expected to be done and the time it will take to do it
- Some indication of probable costs, expected recoveries, problems expected to be solved, and needs expected to be met

The initial plan should be refined, modified, corrected, and detailed as appropriate over time.

There are numerous possible variations in the sequence in which different improvement steps are initiated. One way is through early development of a comprehensive financial management information system. This will ordinarily require a substantial investment of funds and staff time.

The following are some of the considerations which should be reflected in the development of a plan and strategy:

- Avoid taking on more at any one time than can be done effectively.
- Individual steps are more likely to be productive if they are concentrated on specific operations or agencies.
- Governmentwide approaches often tend to spread the effort too thinly to produce early results.
- Give priority to areas and agencies where there are recognized problems or opportunities.

Where to Start

The best place to begin a serious effort to improve the performance of the financial management system will vary with the problems, opportunities, and resources of the particular local government. Some of the possible strategies are briefly described:

- *The Financial Management Information System (FMIS).* The fiscal crisis in New York City and a critical GAO report on Washington, D.C. led those cities to make the huge investment needed to develop a comprehensive FMIS. Other local governments have taken this approach without the impetus of a crisis simply because it seemed the logical way to begin. It is, as chapter 8 indicates, likely to be both expensive and challenging—but it does build the information base needed for most other financial management.
- *One Agency at a Time.* Working with the operating agencies one (or a few) at a time makes the job more manageable and makes it easier to interrelate new approaches in accounting, budgeting, and performance management. Agencies with supportive administrators and competent staff can be identified and the system debugged on the basis of experience in the pilot agencies. However, this approach means that the central budget and accounting agencies must accommodate to two different systems—the new structure in the pilot agencies and the old methods in all other agencies.
- *Budget First.* Usually, first attention has been given to modernizing the budget. This approach focuses on and, usually, achieves an early improvement in decision making and develops a more sophisticated view of needs for changes in other financial management functions. Unfortunately, often system reform has stopped with the improvement of budgeting.
- *Audit as a Beginning.* Boston began with a comprehensive independent audit. This produced a bill of particulars on needs to improve the financial management system. The auditor's recommendations commanded a high degree of credibility because of both the independent position of the audit and the relationship between audit findings and the status of the city in the financial markets. Some

chief executives would, however, be uncomfortable with a public exposure of financial management problems.

- *Performance Management.* Concentrating initially on performance measurement places the attention and the opportunity for improvment on service programs where legislative and citizen interest is likely to be higher than on seemingly more technical and esoteric improvements in accounting and budgeting.
- *Project-by-Project.* It is quite possible to initiate financial management with a series of projects that are not necessarily closely related—so long as the local government has some plan as to how they will all, eventually, fit together. The advantage of this approach is that it permits the locality to maximize its opportunities, concentrating its early efforts in areas where budgetary savings are likely, or where politically important problems are addressed, or where agency leadership is especially supportive, or where federal or state financial assistance is available. The basic disadvantage is the increased difficulty of integrating these dispersed efforts into an overall program.

Cost and Benefits

The most substantial outlays in building an integrated financial management system are those required for the financial management information system. Additional expenditures can be expected in smaller amounts for staff and consultants to develop the program performance management. The amounts will vary among local governments depending upon their size and the current condition of the financial management system. The added expenditures can be distributed over a number of years varying with the speed of the program.

The benefits to be gained are of several different kinds:

- Budgetary savings
- Improvements in program performance
- Improved status in the financial markets
- Increased capacity to predict and avoid possible future fiscal problems

Few of these benefits will be achieved automatically. Most will require management effort to realize the opportunities offered by the system.

Budgetary Savings

Let us begin with the prospects for budgetary saving. There are, first, those opportunities for saving that are related to the installation of a sophisticated financial management information system. These include the following:

- *Indirect cost reimbursement.* A fully developed system for identifying and allocating indirect costs (including depreciation) will often generate a substantial increase in the amounts chargeable under federal and state grant programs and other activities reimbursable from fees, charges, or intergovernmental payments.
- *Cash management.* A program to minimize idle cash balances in checking accounts can be expected to generate increases in interest earnings or reductions in interest expense ranging up to perhaps as much as one half of 1 percent of the total budget.
- *Receivables management.* Similarly, improved tracking of taxes, grants and other receivables, prompter billing, and speedier follow-up of delinquencies will tend to reduce payment lags, increase revenues, and reduce interest costs or increase interest earnings.
- *Full cost pricing.* A review of user charges and fees against the full costs of providing the services involved is likely to suggest the need for increases if costs are to be recovered. Of course, the economic case for an increase may not prove to be politically acceptable.

The savings possible in these functions would be very large in many local governments. They are small, however, in comparison with the potential savings through more efficient management of local programs and services. With improved performance and financial data, increased program and management analysis, and managerial performance targets, savings on the order of 10 percent or more are possible in the larger work force components in the average local government.

However, even after more productive methods are identified, implementation often poses serious problems. Changes may face opposition from employee unions, workers, middle management and, even, program clients. It may also be difficult to obtain appropriations for new equipment or added staff where these are required. Yet, a broad enough management improvement program should, even in the short run, achieve some significant gains in some programs even though progress is blocked, in other areas. A sustained program should, over the long run, be able to achieve nearly all of its objectives.

Improved Performance

The potential for service quality and higher program effectiveness is much like that for budgetary savings. Indeed, in some programs and operations, increased productivity in some activities is needed to provide the manpower required for better service in other activities. A good example is the effort made by a number of local governments to reduce the time spent by police officers in court as a means of increasing police patrol strength.

Improved Fiscal Status

There is little doubt that many local governments can enhance their standing in the financial markets through a first rate financial management system. The bond rating services have responded favorably to presentations by many local governments that detail factors not wholly reflected in routine economic and fiscal data. The difference in interest costs on subsequent bond issues from a one-level upgrading under current conditions would be roughly one quarter of 1 percent.

Increased Control and Predictability

The fiscal crises that many cities encountered during the 1970s were usually rooted in the gradual deterioration over a period of years in an already marginal financial situation. The details were rarely fully evident from financial reports and, sometimes, not fully known to the principal officials of the city. Evaluation was hindered by the uncertain collectibility of delinquent taxes, grants receivable, and other assets supporting short-term borrowing. The potential sensitivity of income elastic taxes to major economic decline had rarely been fully explored by the locality. The possible range of added expenditure requirements from such programs as public assistance and medicaid was not known. The low level of knowledge and anticipation was, hence, a reflection of poor and limited information and a lack of analytical attention to the issues. Both of these would be corrected under the approach outlined in this guide.

It still may not be possible to predict crises; it is, however, entirely practical to identify and chronicle increasing vulnerability to crises.

Getting Help

The various national organizations and associations of local governments, local officials, and certain local agencies have long provided information, technical assistance, and training to their members. The Department of Housing and Urban Development has made grants to several of these organizations and associations to provide additional services under the HUD Financial Management Capacity Sharing Program (FMCS).

The *Financial Management Resource Center* of the Municipal Finance Officers Association (MFOA) is the national contact point for technical support under the FMCS program. The center locates, assesses, and makes available current financial management information to HUD, public interest groups, and other organizations providing training and technical assistance to state and local officials. It will provide agendas, experts, publications, and audio-visuals for state and regional conference sponsors. The center's basic services include the following:

- Financial management library of resource materials, annotated bibliographies, and research publications
- Quick response research and fact sheets to fill gaps in available financial management literature
- Bimonthly newsletter, *Resources in Review,* with reviews of recent publications, updates on recent events, and a calendar of upcoming meeting and training sessions in financial management
- Financial management experts to provide consultation, limited training, and technical services to state and local governments
- Inquiry services: Call (202) 466-2494

Training and technical assistance providers, public interest group representatives, and HUD staff may use the inquiry service to get assistance for state and local financial management problems. Local officials are encouraged to participate in the Resource Center through their public interest groups.

The *International City Management Association* (ICMA) is identifying exemplary financial management practices in small and medium-sized localities, conducting workshops to screen and assess projects and assist their transfer, and publishing the most useful practices. Topics covered include, among others, forecasting, fiscal policy analysis, capital improvement programming, and performance measurement.

In addition, ICMA has developed a financial planning training package including resource materials ("how to's," case studies, etc.) and directions to trainers on how to use the materials. The package covers four steps in a financial planning system: (1) evaluating current financial condition; (2) evaluating future financial condition; (3) developing financial performance targets; and (4) evaluating financial impact of new policy decisions.

The ICMA has also published a list of exemplary practices of small and medium-sized jurisdictions, and has developed concepts and peer match programs to facilitate the transfer of successful techniques from one unit of government to another.

The *U.S. Conference of Mayors* has established the *Mayor's Financial Policy Center,* funded by HUD's FMCS program. The center's first product was the *Mayor's Financial Management Handbook,* published in February 1980.

The *National League of Cities* has prepared, under the FMCS program, resource packages on five financial management issues confronting local governments. The NCL has also published a manual, *Making Sense Out of Dollars: Economic Analysis for Local Government.*

Public Technology, Inc. and the *Urban Consortium* have conducted workshops and prepared the following publications:

- "Multi-Year Revenue and Expenditure Forecasting: The State-of-the-Practice in Large Urban Jurisdictions"
- "Effectiveness Measures: Literature and Practice Review"

The *Academy for Contemporary Problems* has taken over the responsibilities of the *National Training and Development Service* (NTDS), a nonprofit organization created to help increase the problem-solving capabilities of state, county, and municipal officials. The Academy administers the Trainers Resource Exchange, an FMCS clearinghouse for financial management trainers and assistance providers, and, in addition, publishes catalogues of financial management training resources, a directory of state and local government trainers in financial management, and the bimonthly report, *Resource Briefs*, a review of training programs. There is also a telephone inquiry service (202-628-0060) to answer specific training-related questions.

The *National Association of Counties* (NACO) has prepared a series of resource packages for policy makers on the following five topics:

- Tax Limits: problems with managing tax limitations and expenditure reductions at a time of spiraling costs and growing service demand
- Mandates: learning to cope with state and federal legislative and administrative mandates
- Pensions: pension liabilities, management of the pension plan, and setting local pension policies
- Forecasting: reliability of revenue and expenditure forecasts for the annual budget, or for estimating the fiscal impacts of current or proposed policies.
- Mayor's Role: support for the mayor in overseeing accounting, debt management and policy, analysis of pension liability, and coping with inflation/recession

The resource packages present relevant issues, effective policies and practices, resources for further assistance, a glossary of terms, and an annotated bibliography.

Another service provided by NACO is the Exchange, a national clearinghouse of up-to-date information and improved management practices for county officials. Assistance is provided in three areas:

- General management of all operations of county government, in-

cluding county structure and home rule as well as day-to-day administrative activities
- Financial management and improvements in fiscal operations
- Labor-management including personnel practices and employee benefits

The *Council of State Community Affairs Agencies* (COSCAA) is the national organization representing the state agencies responsible for local assistance functions in housing, community development, economic development, planning, training, and technical assistance. The council has produced and disseminated, under the FMCS program, the *State Financial Management Resource Guide* and *DCA Roles in Local Government Financial Management: Ten State Profiles.* These publications provide useful guidance on the extent to which local governments are likely to find assistance in their own states.

The Joint Center for Political Studies (JCPS) is a nonprofit, nonpartisan, tax-exempt organization formed in 1970 to advance effective minority group participation in the political process. JCPS has undertaken an FMCS demonstration project to provide financial management training and technical assistance to officials from disadvantaged communities.

The assistance available through guides, manuals, training packages, workshops and training programs under the FMCS program is extensive. Additional resources catalogued in the various FMCS publications are available through other organizations such as the state universities, the state associations of local governments, and the various state departments of community affairs.

One important aspect of the work done under the FMCS program has been the identification of many local governments with exemplary practices in local financial management. A number of these local governments are, for example, cited in the exhibits used in this publication. There is no better way of learning the problems, the possible pitfalls, the costs and benefits of integrating financial management than to visit a local government with similar characteristics that has already done it.

Summing Up: Integrating Your Financial Management Systems

This guide describes what may seem on first reading to many local officials a demanding set of challenges. But if there's any single message we want to get across, it's this: there are appropriate starting points toward an integrated financial management system for any community—however large or small, however simple or sophisticated its current financial systems.

You don't need to do it all at once. And however far you may think your financial systems are from the ideal, there are almost certainly other communities that start out in even worse shape.

As you move along you'll begin to forge the linkages among the separate financial functions that are the hallmark of an integrated system. These will provide better information for better decisions, better decisions for better public services. That's what financial system integration is all about.

Bibliography

General Financial Management Publications

Anthony, Robert N., and Herzlinger, Regina. *Management Control in Non-Profit Organizations.* Irwin, 1977.

*Aronson, J. Richard. *Municipal Fiscal Indicators: Urban Consortium Information Bulletin of the Management, Finance and Resource Task Force.* Public Technology, Inc., August 1980.

Aronson, J. Richard, and Schwartz, Eli (Eds.). *Management Policies in Local Government Finance.* Washington, D.C.: International City Management Association, 1975.

Bohnsaek, Jim."EDP: An Organizational Question." *Governmental Finance,* Vol. 6, No. 3, August 1977.

*Galambos, Eva C., and Schreiber, Arthur F. *Making Sense Out of Dollars: Economic Analysis for Local Governments.* National League of Cities, 1978.

Golembiewski, Robert T., Ed. *Public Budgeting and Finance: Readings in Theory and Practice.* Itasca, Illinois: F. E. Peacock Publishers, 1968.

*Government Finance Research Center, *Government Financial Management Resources in Review.* Washington, D.C.: Municipal Finance Officers Association, Bimonthly.

Granville Corporation. *Final Report on the National Conference on Local Government's Priority Needs for Financial Management Capacity Sharing,* February 1981.

*Granville Corporation. *Local Financial Management in the 80's: Techniques for Responding to the New Fiscal Realities.* Report of the June 1979 Conference on Local Financial Management, January 1980.

Hanson, Phillip. "Evaluating Data Processing Alternatives." *Governmental Finance,* Vol. 6, No. 3, August 1977.

*Harrell, Rhett. *Developing a Financial Management Information System: The Key Issues.* Summary Report. Municipal Finance Officers Association, November 1980.

*International City Management Association, Local Government Financial Management Handbooks. *Handbook 1: Evaluating Financial Condition* by Sanford Groves, 1980.

Handbook 2: Financial Trend Monitoring System by Sanford Groves, 1980.

Handbook 3: Financial Jeopardy by Maureen W. Godsey, 1980.

Handbook 4: Financial Performance Goals by Maureen W. Godsey.

Handbook 5: Tools for Making Financial Decisions by Maureen W. Godsey.

*International City Management Association, *Current Approaches to Financial Management: A Directory of Practices,* Spring 1980.

International City Management Association, *Elected Officials Handbook: Series 1—Financial Management,* 1977.

Kraemer, Kenneth L., Dutton, William H., and Northrop, Alana. *The Management of Information Systems: Implementation Policy for Computing in American Local Government.* Public Policy Research Organization, University of California, Irvine, CA, October 1978.

Kraemer, Kenneth L., and King, John Leslie. "Financial Management Systems: Independent and Integrated Design," in *Computers in Local Government: Finance and Administration,* Auerbach Publishers Inc., Pennsauken, N.J., 1980.

Kraemer, Kenneth L., and King, John Leslie. "Integrated Financial Management Systems: Dayton Case Study," in *Computers in Local Government: Finance and Administration,* Auerbach Publishers Inc., Pennsauken, N.J., 1980.

Lodal, Jan M. "Improving Local Government Financial Information Systems." *Duke Law Journal,* Vol. 1976, No. 6, 1977.

Lindholm, Richard W., and Wignjowijoto, Hartojo. *Financing and Managing State and Local Government.* Lexington, Mass.: D.C. Heath & Co., 1979.

McFarlan, F. Warren, and Nolan, Richard. *Information Systems Handbook.* Homewood, Ill., 1975.

Moak, Lennox L., and Hillhouse, Albert M. *Concepts and Practices in Local Government Finance.* Chicago: Municipal Finance Officers Association, 1975.

*Municipal Finance Officers Association, Government Finance Research Center, *Introduction to the Elements of Financial Management.* Washington, D.C., 1978.

Musgrave, Richard A., and Musgrave, Peggy B. *Public Finance in Theory and Practice.* New York: McGraw Hill Book Company, 1973.

*National Academy of Public Administration. *Improving Financial Management in State and Local Government: An Assessment of a HUD Capacity Sharing Program.* November 1980.

Peterson, John E., Spain, Catherine L., and Laffey, Martharose. *State and Local Government Finance and Financial Management: A Compendium of Current Research.* Washington, D.C.: Government Finance Research Center, 1978.

*Peterson, John E., Stallings, Wayne C., and Spain, Catherine L. *State Roles in Local Government Financial Management.* Municipal Finance Officers Association, 1979.

*Peterson, John E., Stallings, Wayne C., and Spain, Catherine L. *State Roles in Local Government Financial Management: Nine Case Studies.* Municipal Finance Officers Association, 1979.

Rapp, Brian W., and Patitucci, Frank M. *Managing Local Government for Improved Performance.* Boulder, Colorado: Westview Press, 1977.

Rosenberg, Phillip, and Stallings, Wayne C. *Is Your City Heading for Financial Difficulty? A Guidebook.* Municipal Finance Officers Association.

Rosenberg, Phillip, and Stallings, Wayne C. *A Guidebook to Improved Financial Management for Small Cities and Other Government Units.* Municipal Finance Officers Association, 1979.

Rosenbloom, Richard S., and Russell, John (Eds.). *New Urban Management: Studies in System and Organizational Analysis.* Boston: Harvard Business School, 1971.

Ross, Bernard H., Ed. *Urban Management: A Guide to Information Sources.* Detroit: Gale Research Co., 1979.

Snyder, James C. *Fiscal Management and Planning in Local Government.* Lexington, Mass.: D.C. Heath and Company, 1977.

Stallings, Wayne C. "Integrated Financial Management Systems: Key Features and Implementation Considerations," in *Computers in Local Government: Finance and Administration,* Auerbach Publishers, Inc., Pennsauken, N.J., 1980.

*U.S. Conference of Mayors. *A Mayors' Financial Management Handbook.* February 1980.
*U.S. Department of Housing and Urban Development and the National Training and Development Service. *Final Conference Report of the National Conference on the Financial Management Needs of Local Governments, Local Government Financial Management Capacity Sharing Program.* June 1978.
*U.S. Department of Housing and Urban Development. *Financial Management Capacity Sharing Program, 1979 Annual Report.* February 1980.
U.S. Department of Housing and Urban Development, Office of Policy Development and Research. *Selected Implementation Bibliography of Research Publications for State and Local Governments.* Washington, D.C., 1979.
Urban Management Curriculum Development Project. *Policy Program Analyses and Evaluation Techniques.* Washington, D.C.: National Training and Development Service, 1978.

Budgeting

Anthony, Robert N. "Zero Based Budgeting is a Fraud." *Wall Street Journal* April 27, 1977, p. 26.
Anton, Thomas J. "Budgeting in Three Illinois Cities." *Commission Papers of the Institute of Government and Public Affairs.* University of Illinois, Urbana, 1964.
Aronson, Richard J., and Schwartz, Eli. "Capital Budgeting." *Management Policies in Local Government,* Aronson and Schwartz, eds., Washington, D.C.: International City Management Association, 1975.
Bahl, Roy W., and Gustely, Richard. "Forecasting Urban Government Expenditures." Paper presented at the *Sixty-Seventh Conference of the National Tax Association,* Syracuse, N.Y.: Maxwell School of Citizenship and Public Affairs, October 1974.
Bahl, Roy, and Monthrone, William. *Forecasting Municipal Revenues and Expenditures.* Washington, D.C.: Coalition of Northeast Municipalities, January 1980.
Bahl, Roy, and Schroeder, Larry. *Occasional Paper No. 38, Forecasting Local Government Budgets.* Syracuse, N.Y.: Metropolitan Studies Program, December 1979.
*Bahl, Roy, and Schroeder, Larry. *Bibliography: Revenue and Expenditure Forecasting in Local Government.* Syracuse, N.Y.: Metropolitan Studies Program, June 1978.
Blodgett, Terrell. "Zero Base Budgeting Systems: Seventeen Steps to Success." National Civic Review, Vol. 67, No. 3, March 1978.
Borut, Daniel J. "Implementing PPBS: A Practitioner's Viewpoint." *Financing the Metropolis,* John P. Crecine, ed., Beverly Hills, California: Sage Publications, 1970.
Burkhead, Jess. *Government Budgeting.* New York: John Wiley & Sons, 1956.

*Note: Items preceded by an asterisk were produced under the auspices of HUD's Financial Management Capacity Sharing Program.

Burkhead, Jesse, and Bringewatt, Paul. *Municipal Budgeting: A Primer for Elected Officials.* Washington, D.C.: Joint Center for Political Studies, 1974.

Cleaveland, James R. "Local Government Retrenchment and Zero Base Budgeting." *Experiences in Zero Base Budgeting,* Joseph L. Herbert, ed., New York: P.B.I., 1977.

Craemer, Robert M. "Local Government Expenditure Forecasting." *Governmental Finance,* Vol. 7, No. 4, November 1978.

Crecine, John P. *Government Problem Solving: A Computer Simulation of Municipal Budgeting.* Chicago: Rand McNally & Company, 1968.

Friedman, Lewis B. *Budgeting Municipal Expenditures.* New York: Praeger Publishers, 1975.

Fukuhara, Rackham S. "Zero Base Budgeting: Some City Experiences." *Management Information Service,* Vol. 10, No. 1, 1978.

George Washington University, State-Local Finances Project, *Implementing PPB in State, City and County.* Washington, D.C., June 1969.

Grossbard, Stephen I. *PPBS for State and Local Officials.* Kingston, Rhode Island: University of Rhode Island, Bureau of Government Research, Research Series No. 15, 1971.

Grossman, David A. *The Future of New York City's Capital Plant.* Washington, D.C.: The Urban Institute, 1979.

Hale, George F., and Douglas, Scott R. "The Politics of Budget Execution: Financial Manipulation in State and Local Government." *Administration and Society,* Vol. 9, No. 3, November 1977.

*Haskins and Sells, Government Services Group. *Implementing Effective Cash Management in Local Government: A Practical Guide.* 1977.

Hayes, Frederick O'R. *Creative Budgeting in New York City.* Washington, D.C.: The Urban Institute, 1971.

Hirsch, Werner Z., et. al. *Local Government Program Budgeting: Theory and Practice.* New York: Praeger Publishers, 1974.

Howe, George F. "Developing a Capital Improvements Program." *Management Information Service,* Vol. 1, No. 9-3, March 1969.

Hyde, Albert C., and Shafritz, Jay M., eds. *Government Budgeting: Theory, Process, Politics.* Oak Park, Illinois, Moore Publishing Co., 1978.

Kelley, Joseph T. "Allocation Criteria in Budgeting." *Governmental Finance,* Vol. 7, No. 3, August 1978.

Key, V. O. "The Lack of a Budget Theory." *American Political Science Review,* Vol. 34, No. 4, December 1940.

Kimmel, Wayne A., et al. *Municipal Management and Budget Methods: An Evaluation of Policy Research.* Washington, D.C.: The Urban Institute, 1974.

*Kossak, Shelley. *Bridging the Gap.* National Association of Counties, 1980 (55 pp.).

Lee, Robert D., Jr., and Johnson, Donald W. *Public Budgeting Systems,* second edition. Baltimore: University Park Press, 1977.

Leininger, David L., and Wong, Ronald C. "Zero Base Budgeting in Garland, Texas." *Management Information Report,* Vol. 8, No. 4A, April 1976.

Lindholm, Richard W., Arnold, David S., and Herbert, Richard R. "The Budgetary Process." *Management Policies in Local Government Finance,* J. Richard Aronson and Eli Schwartz, eds., Washington, D.C.: The International City Management Association, 1975.

Lynden, Fremont J., and Miller, Ernest G. *Planning, Programming, Budgeting: A Systems Approach to Management,* 2nd edition. Chicago: Rand McNally, 1972.

Meltsner, Arnold J., and Wildavsky, Aaron. "Leave City Budgeting Alone!: A Survey, Case Study and Recommendations for Reform." *Financing The Metropolis,* John P. Crecine, ed., Beverly Hills: Page Publications Inc., 1970.

Minmier, George S., and Hermanson, Roger. "A Look at Zero-Base Budgeting— The Georgia Experience." *Atlanta Economic Review,* Vol. 26, No. 4, 1976.

Moak, Lennox L., and Killian, Kathryn W. *A Manual of Techniques for the Preparation, Consideration, Adoption, and Administration of Operating Budgets.* Chicago: Municipal Finance Officers Association, 1973.

Maok, Lennox L., and Gordon, Kathryn Killian. *Budgeting for Smaller Governmental Units.* Chicago: Municipal Finance Officers Association, 1965.

Moak, Lennox L. "The Trouble with Revenue Sources." *Governmental Finance,* Vol. 6, No. 4, November 1977.

Mushkin, Selma J. "PPB for the Cities: Problems and the Next Steps." *Financing The Metropolis,* John P. Crecine, Ed., Beverly Hills: Sage Publications, 1970.

National League of Cities. *Capital Improvements Programming: A Guide for Small Cities, Towns, Boroughs, and Counties.* Washington, D.C., 1968.

Novick, David, ed. *Program Budgeting: Program Analysis and the Federal Budget.* Cambridge, Mass.: Harvard University Press, 1965.

*Patittuci, Frank M., and Lichtenstein, Frank M. *Improving Cash Management in Local Government: A Comprehensive Review.* Municipal Finance Officers Association, 1977.

*Public Technology, Inc. *Multi-Year Revenue and Expenditure Forecasting: Report of National Workshops,* August 1980.

Pyhrr, Peter A. "The Zero Base Approach to Government Budgeting." *Public Administration Review,* Vol. 37, No. 1, January/February, 1977.

Reinhart, George W. "A Local Government Budgetary Process." *Management Information Service,* Vol. 10, No. 1, 1978.

Sarant, Peter C. *Zero Base Budgeting in the Public Sector.* Reading, Mass.: Addison-Wesley Publishing Company, 1978.

Schick, Allen. *Budget Innovation in the States.* Washington, D.C.: The Brookings Institution, 1971.

Schick, Allen. "The Road to PPB: The Stages of Budget Reform." *Public Administration Review,* Vol. 26, No. 4, December 1966.

Sonenblum, Sidney. *The Environment Facing Local Government Program Budgeting.* Los Angeles: University of California, Institute of Government and Public Affairs, 1973.

Stallings, Wayne. "Improved Budget Communications in Smaller Local Governments." *Governmental Finance,* Vol. 7, No. 3, August 1978.

Streiss, Alan Walter. *Local Government Finance.* Lexington, Mass.: D.C. Heath & Company, 1975.

The Urban Consortium and Public Technology, Inc., Multi-Year Revenue and Expenditure Forecasting: The State of Practice in Large Urban Jurisdictions, July 1979.

White, Michael J. "Budget Policy: Where Does it Begin and End? *Governmental Finance,* Vol. 7, No. 3, August 1978.

Wildavsky, Aaron. *The Politics of the Budgetary Process,* 2nd edition. Boston: Little Brown and Company, 1974.
Worthley, John A., and Ludwin, William G., eds. *Zero Base Budgeting in State and Local Government.* New York: Praeger Publishers, 1979.

Accounting

Anthony, Robert N. *Financial Accounting in Nonbusiness Organizations.* Stamford, Connecticut: Financial Accounting Standards Board, 1978.
Caldwell, Kenneth S. "The Accounting Aspects of Budgetary Reform." *Governmental Finance,* Vol. 7, No. 3, August 1978.
Chait, Edward P. "The Reevaluation of GAAP for State and Local Governments." *Government Accountants Journal,* Vol. 27, No. 2, Summer 1978.
Cheng, Phillip C. "Accounting for Small Municipalities in North Carolina: An Empirical Study." *Government Accountants Journal,* Vol. 26, No. 1, Spring 1977.
Enke, Ernest. "Municipal Accounting." *Management Policies in Local Government Finance,* J. Richard Aronson and Eli Schwartz, eds., Washington, D.C.: International City Management Association, 1975.
Enke, Ernest. "The Accounting Preconditions of PPB(s)." *Management Accountancy,* Vol. 53, January 1972.
Ernst & Whitney. *How Cities Can Improve Their Financial Reporting.* Cleveland, Ernst & Whitney, 1979.
Freeman, Robert F. "New Thoughts in Governmental Accounting." *Governmental Finance,* Vol. 1, No. 4, November 1972.
Hass, Richard J. *Improving the Annual Financial Report.* Chicago: Municipal Finance Officers Association, January 1978.
Harrill, E. Reese, et. al. "Famis" A Financial Accounting and Management Information System for Local Government." *Management Controls,* Vol. 2, No. 5, 1974.
Hay, Leon E., and Mikesell, R. M. *Government Accounting.* Homewood, Illinois: Richard D. Unwin, Inc., 1974.
Lynn, Edward S., and Freeman, Robert J. *Fund Accounting: Theory and Practice.* Englewood Cliffs, N.J.: Prentice-Hall, 1974.
Municipal Finance Officers Association. *Accounting Systems for Revenue Sharing.* Chicago: MFOA, 1974.
Municipal Finance Officers Association. *An Accounting Handbook for Small Cities and Other Governmental Units,* 1979.
National Council on Government Accounting. *Governmental Accounting Auditing and Financial Reporting* (GAAFR). Chicago: Municipal Finance Officers Association, revised edition, 1979.
Potts, James H. "Some Highlights in the Evolution of the Fund Concept in Municipal Accounting." *The Government Accountants Journal,* Vol. 26, No. 2, Summer 1977.
Rau, Kailas J. "Development and Regulation of Standards: Municipal Accounting and Reporting." *The Government Accountants Journal,* Vol. 27, No. 4, Winter, 1978–79.

Schramm, John E., Jr. "Municipal Accounting and Reporting." The CPA Journal, Vol. 46, Nos. 5 and 6, 1976. Reprinted in *Readings in Governmental and Non-Profit Accounting*, Richard J. Vargo, ed., Belmont, California: Wadsworth Publishing Company 1977.

Still, John F. *Local Government Accounting Developments: An Overview*. Chicago: Municipal Finance Officers Association, November 1971.

U.S. Department of the Treasury, Office of Revenue Sharing. *Audit Guide and Standards for Revenue Sharing Recipients*. Washington, D.C., 1973.

Performance Management

Barbour, George P., Jr. "Improving Productivity: A View from the Council Chamber." *Management Information Service Report*, Vol. 8, No. 6, June 1976.

Committee for Economic Development. *Improving Productivity in State and Local Government*. New York: March 1976.

*City of Dallas. *Improving Productivity and Decision-Making Through the Use of Effectiveness Measures*. Dallas, Texas, 1979.

Connellan, Thomas K. "Management by Objectives in Local Government: A System of Organizational Leadership." *Management Information Service* Report, Vol. 7, No.2A, February 1975.

Crane, Edgar G., et. al. *State Government Productivity*. New York: Praeger Publishers, 1976.

Cummings, Thomas G. *Improving Productivity and the Quality of Work Life*. New York: Praeger Publishers, 1977.

Davis, Robert H. "Measuring the Effectiveness of Municipal Services." *Management Information Service*, Vol. 2, No. LS-8, August 1970.

DeVivo, Thomas G. "Productivity Improvement: Its Impact and Importance." *Governmental Finance*, Vol. 4, No. 1, February 1975.

*Epstein, Paul. *Using Performance Measures in Local Government: A Guide to Improve Decisions, Performance and Accountability*. Washington, D.C.: U.S. Department of Housing and Urban Development, April 1981.

Fabricant, Solomon. *A Primer on Productivity*. New York: Random House, 1969.

Fisk, Donald M. "Issues in Local Government Productivity Measurement." *Public Management*, Vol. 56, No. 6, June 1974.

Fosler, R. Scott. "State and Local Productivity and the Public Sector." *Public Administration Review*, Vol. 38, No. 1, January/February 1978.

Friedman, Lewis, and Martin, John T. "Rating Cities' Performance." *National Civic Review*, January 1976.

Fukuhara, Rackham S. "Improving Effectiveness: Responsive Public Services." *Municipal Management Innovation Series, No. 10*, International City Management Association, Washington, D.C., 1976.

Greiner, John M.; Dahl, Roger E.; Hatry, Harry P.; Millar, Annie P. *Monetary Incentives and Work Standards in Five Cities: Impacts and Implications for Management and Labor*. Washington, D.C.: The Urban Institute, 1977.

Greiner, J., and Hatry, Harry O. *Managing Human Resources in Local Government: A Survey of Employee Incentive Plans*. Washington, D.C.: National Commission on Productivity, October 1973.

*Greiner, John M., and Hatry, Harry P. *Productivity and Motivation: A Review of State and Local Government.* Washington, D.C.: The Urban Institute, 1981.

Hall, John R., Jr. *Factors Related to Local Government Effectiveness and Efficiency Measurement.* Washington, D.C.: The Urban Institute, 1978.

Hatry, Harry P. "The Status of Productivity Measurement in the Public Sector." *Public Administration Review,* Vol. 38, No. 1, January/February 1978.

Hatry, Harry P. "Criteria for Evaluation in Planning State and Local Programs." *Planning Programming Budgeting.* Fremont J. Lynden and Ernest G. Miller, eds., Chicago: Rand McNally Publishing Company, 1972.

*Hatry, Harry P., et. al. *Efficiency Measurement for Local Government Services: Some Initial Suggestions.* Washington, D.C.: The Urban Institute, April 1978.

Hatry, Harry P., et. al. *How Effective are Your Community Services?: Procedures for Monitoring the Effectiveness of Municipal Services.* Washington, D.C.: The Urban Institute, 1977.

Hatry, Harry P. *Performance Measurement Principles and Techniques: An Overview for Local Governments.* Washington, D.C.: U.S. Department of Housing and Urban Development, Office of Policy Development and Research, 1981.

Hatry, Harry P., and Fisk, Donald M. *Improving Productivity and Productivity Measurement in Local Government.* Washington, D.C.: National Commission on Productivity, June 1971.

Haveman, Robert H., and Margolis, Julius, eds. *Public Expenditures and Policy Analysis.* Chicago: Markham Publishing Company, 1970.

Hayes, Frederick O'R. *Productivity in Local Government.* Lexington, Mass.: D.C. Heath and Company, 1977.

Holzer, Marc. "The Demand for Productivity in the Municipal Civil Service." *Public Administration Review,* Vol. 37, No. 5, September/October 1977.

Horton, Raymond D. "Productivity and Productivity Bargaining in Government: A Critical Analysis." *Public Administration Review,* July/August, 1976.

John Wiley and Sons, Inc., *Productivity Improvement Handbook for State and Local Government."* New York, 1980.

Keller, Lawrence E. "Performance Measures, Systems, and Local Government." *Public Productivity Review,* December 1975.

Kuper, George H. "Productivity Improvement: The Route to More Effective Public Management." *Public Management,* Vol. 56, No. 6, June 1974.

Mark, Jerome A. "Progress in Measuring Productivity in Government." *Monthly Labor Review,* Vol. 45, December 1972.

*National Academy of Public Administration, *Productivity Improvement Handbook for State and Local Government.* April 1980.

National Center for Productivity and Quality of Working Life, *Improving Productivity and Productivity Measurement in Local Governments.* Washington, D.C.: 1971.

National Center for Productivity and Quality of Working Life. "MBO Changes Managerial Attitudes in Charlotte, North Carolina." *Improving Governmental Productivity: Selected Case Studies.* Washington, D.C., 1977.

National Commission on Productivity and Work Quality. *Improving Municipal*

Productivity: Work Measurement for Better Management, Washington, D.C., November 1975.

National Commission on Productivity and Work Quality. *Employee Incentives to Improve State and Local Productivity.* Washington, D.C., March 1975.

National Commission on Productivity and Work Quality. *A Jurisdictional Guide to Public Sector Productivity Improvement Projects.* Washington, D.C., 1975.

Price Waterhouse and Co. *Productivity Improvement Manual for Local Government Officials.* New York: Price Waterhouse and Co., 1977.

*Public Technology, Inc. *Effectiveness Measures: Literature and Practice Review.* Washington, D.C., 1979.

Public Technology, Inc. *Performance Measurement and Improvement of Local Services: Proceedings of National Workshops.* August 1980.

*Rhode Island Department of Community Affairs. *Performance Measurement and Cost Accounting for Smaller Local Governments* (undated).

Ross, John P., and Burkhead, Jessie. *Productivity in the Local Government Sector.* Lexington, Mass.: D.C. Heath and Company, 1974.

Schwarz, Christine. *Goal Setting by the Governing Body: The Why and How.* International City Management Association, Washington, D.C.

*Thomas, John. *So. Mr. Mayor, You Want to Improve Productivity.* Washington, D.C.: National Commission on Productivity, 1974.

U.S. Department of Housing and Urban Development. *Current Approaches to Financial Management.* Washington, D.C.

U.S. Department of Housing and Urban Development, Office of Policy Development and Research. *Improving Productivity of Neighborhood Services: A Washington, D.C. Case Study.* Washington, D.C., November 1978.

U.S. Department of Housing and Urban Development, Office of Policy Development and Research. *Improving Productivity and Decision-Making Through the Use of Effectiveness Measures.* Washington, D.C., February 1979.

*U.S. Department of Housing and Urban Development, Office of Policy Development and Research. *Summary of Productivity Improvement Projects.* Washington, D.C., May 1970.

U.S. Department of Housing and Urban Development. *Managing with Performance Measures in Local Government: A Dialogue.* Washington, D.C., 1979.

U.S. Department of Housing and Urban Development, Office of Policy Development and Research. *Practical Ideas for the Government That Has Everything— Including Productivity Problems.* Washington, D.C., May 1979.

*U.S. Department of Housing and Urban Development and Research. *Practical Ideas for Governments Facing Planning and Scheduling Problems,* 1979.

*U.S. Department of Housing and Urban Development, Office of Policy Development and Research. *Practical Ideas for Small Governments Facing Big Problems,* 1979.

*U.S. Department of Housing and Urban Development, Office of Policy Development and Research. *Practical Ideas on Ways for Governments to Work Together,* 1979.

*U.S. Department of Housing and Urban Development, Office of Policy Development and Research. *Summary of Productivity Improvement Projects,* 1979.

U.S. Department of Labor, Bureau of Labor Statistics. "Concepts and Measures of Productivity," and "The Meaning of Productivity." Bulletin No. 1714, Washington, D.C., 1971.

U.S. Department of Labor, Bureau of Statistics. *Productivity: A Bibliography.* Bulletin No. 1514, Washington, D.C., 1966.

U.S. General Accounting Office. *Federal Productivity: Methods Measurement Results.* Washington, D.C., August 1972.

U.S. Office of Management and Budget, Joint Financial Management Program, Government Productivity, 001.1. *Productivity Trends and Current Efforts.* Washington, D.C., July 1976.

The Urban Institute. *The Challenge of Productivity Diversity: Improving Local Government Productivity Measurement and Evaluation.* Washington, D.C.: National Commission on Productivity, National Technical Information Service, June 1972.

The Urban Institute. *Measuring The Effectiveness of Basic Municipal Services.* Washington, D.C., 1974.

The Urban Institute in cooperation with the National League of Cities and National Association of Counties. *Performance Measurement, A Guide for Local Elected Officials.* 1980.

Wise, Charles R., and Norton, Orville. *Productivity and Program Evaluation in the Public Sector: An Annotated Bibliography.* Midwest Intergovernmental Training Committee, 1978.

Auditing

American Institute of Certified Public Accountants. *Audits of State and Local Government Units.* New York, 1975.

Atkisson, Robert M., and Chait, Edward P. "The Case for the Internal Auditor in Local Government: The Eyes and Ears of Public Officials and the People." *Governmental Finance,* Vol. 7, No. 3, November 1978.

Cancellieri, Alfred J. *The Expanded Scope of Government Auditing: C & L Reports to Management.* Coopers and Lybrand, 1976.

Coe, Charles. *Guide to Selecting an Outside Auditor.* Athens, Georgia: University of Georgia, Institute of Government, 1977.

Dittenhoffer, Mortimer A. "Internal Auditing: A Help in City Management Functions. *Nations Cities,* July 1971.

Drucker, Meyer. "The Importance of Internal Revenue Review for Local Governments." *Governmental Finance,* Vol. 2, No. 2, No. 1, January 1973. Reprinted in *Readings in Governmental and Non-Profit Accounting,* Richard J. Vargo, ed., Belmont, California: Wadsworth Publishing Company, 1977.

Gary R. Jack. "The Office of Revenue Sharing's Cooperative Federal, State, Local, and Private Enterprise Auditing Program." *Governmental Finance,* Vol. 7, No. 3, August 1978.

Granof, Michael H. "Operational Auditing Standards for Audits of Government Services." *The CPA Journal,* Vol. 43, No.12, 1973.

Hollingsworth, Clark D., and Harker, Betty Jo. "Preparing for the External Auditors." *Governmental Finance,* Vol. 7, No. 3, August 1978.

Knighton, Lennis M. "Information Preconditions of Performance Auditing." *Governmental Finance*, Vol. 5, No. 2, February 1976.

Lundteigen, Paul A. "Expanded Role of the Office of Revenue Sharing in Audits of State and Local Governments." *The Government Accountants Journal*, Vol. 27, No. 3, Fall 1978.

Massachusetts Department of Community Affairs, Office of Local Affairs and Coopers and Lybrand. *The Municipal Audit: Choice and Opportunity*, 1978.

Morse, Ellsworth H., Jr. "Performance and Operational Auditing." *Journal of Accountancy*, Vol. 131, No. 6, 1971. Reprinted in *Readings in Governmental and Non-Profit Accounting*, Richard J. Vargo, ed., Belmont, California: Wadsworth Publishing Company, 1972.

O'-Keefe, Herbert A., Jr. "Performance Audits in Local Government—Benefits, Problems, and Challenges." *Management Information Service Report*, Vol. 8, Special Report, April 1976.

Pomeranz, Felix, et. al. *Auditing in the Public 'Sector*. Boston: Warren, Gorham, and Lamont, 1976.

Price Waterhouse and Company. *Understanding Local Government Financial Statements: A Citizen's Guide*. New York: Price Waterhouse and Company, 1976.

*Rousmaniere, Peter F. *Local Government Auditing*. New York: The Council on Municipal Performance, 1979.

Steinberg, Harold I. "Understanding Municipal Financial Audits." *Management Controls*, Vol. 24, No.1, January/February 1977.

Tierney, Cornelius E. *Governmental Auditing*. Chicago: Commerce Clearing House, Inc., 1979.

Tower, Ralph B., Jr. "Auditing Financial Statements of Local Government Units— How Comparable Are They?" *The Government Accountants Journal*, Vol. 27, No. 3, Fall 1978.

U.S. General Accounting Office. *Auditors—Agents for Good Government*. Audit Standards Series, No. 2, 1973.

U.S. General Accounting Office. *Examples of Findings from Government Audits*. Audit Standards Series, No. 4, 1973.

U.S. General Accounting Office. *Using Auditing to Improve Efficiency and Economy*. Audit Standard Series, No. 7, 1975.

U.S. General Accounting Office. *Standards for Audit of Governmental Organizations, Programs, Activities, and Functions*, 1972.

Yeager, Frank A. "Auditing CETA—An Approach to Intergovernmental Auditing." *The Government Accountants Journal*, Vol. 27, No. 4, Winter, 1978/1979.

Other Useful and Relevant Publications

*Advisory Commission on Intergovernmental Relations, in cooperation with the National Conference of State Legislatures and the National Governor's Association. *Improving Financial Management: An ACIR Project to Promote and Encourage State Initiatives in Local Financial Management Capacity Building*. Washington, D.C., 1979.

*Arenson, Todd, and Eikossak, Shelley. *Pension Issues for Local Policy Makers*.

National League of Cities and National Association of Counties, December 1980.

*Council of State Community Affairs Agencies. *Department of Community Affairs Roles in Local Government Financial Management, Ten State Profiles,* 1978.

Lantrip, Jennifer. *Giving Technical Assistance.* Virginia Municipal League/Virginia Commonwealth University, 1980.

*Municipal Finance Officers Association. *Community Development Block Grant Budgetary and Financial Management: A Guide for Local Government Officials.*

*National Association of Counties. *Living With Mandates: A Guide for Elected Officials.* February 1980.

*National Training and Development Services. *Training in Local Government Financial Management Practices: Volume V TRS Catalog of Resources.* January 1980.

*New York State Assembly, Ways and Means Committee. *Municipal Insurance Pools: An Appropriate Alternative for Local Governments,* January 1980. Also, *Supplement,* January 1981.

*Special Commission, State House, Mass. *Local Mandated Program Inventory Manual,* 1980.

*Valente, Paula R. *Current Approaches to Risk Management: A Directory of Practices.* International City Management Association, November 1980.